The Perils of Being Permanently Seated

A Humorous Look at Life in a Wheelchair

by
Shirley Stinger Watson

Copyright © 2012 Shirley Stinger Watson

All rights reserved. No part of this book may be reproduced or transmitted in any form or by any means, electronic or mechanical, including photocopying, recording, or by any information storage and retrieval system, without permission in writing from the publisher.

Published by Tanya Design + Photo
Liberty Lake, WA 99019
509-230-6676
http://www.tanyasmith.net

Cover and Layout Design: Tanya Goodall Smith

ISBN 978-0-9900139-0-7

First Print Edition

For my Family & Friends

Introduction

When I became a quadriplegic from a car accident at age twenty, I decided I was not going to be defined by my paralysis but would meet my challenges with humor. This narrative is a collection of 55 years of Christmas letters that I wrote to family and friends. I hope as you read, you will laugh along with me.

As you will see, I moved quite often the first twelve years post trauma. During this time, some of my letters were lost; therefore, even though all of these things took place, I may have some in the wrong years. I put them in files in my brain; I just cannot remember which file I put them in. Please forgive!

LONGVIEW DAILY

LONGVIEW, WASHINGTON, SATURDAY, AUGUST 20, 1955

Two Drivers Brush Death As Cars Plunge Off Embankments

Woman Injured Mrs. Shirley Watson, 20, Toledo, suffered a fractured neck when the car she was driving plunged off Pacific Highway down a 150-foot embankment, 3.2 miles north of Kelso, about 4:10 p.m. Friday. Looking at the car is State Patrolman Ernie House. —Daily News photo.

Two persons narrowly escaped death Friday in Cowlitz County when cars they were driving plunged down steep embankments in separate traffic mishaps, the State Patrol reported today.

Injured were Mrs. Shirley Watson, 20, Box 109, Toledo; and Rex K. Watson, 58, Portland, no relation.

Mrs. Watson suffered a fractured neck when the car she was driving crossed the center strip of Pacific Highway, 3.2 miles north of Kelso, tore across two northbound traffic lanes and plunged off a 150-foot embankment.

She was the only person in the car. State Patrolman Ernie House said the car traveled 175 yards before it went over the embankment, taking two traffic control posts with it. The mishap took place about 3:40 p.m.

Witnesses to the accident said they could give no reason for it. Cowlitz County Deputy Sheriff Jack Alton, who happened on the mishap shortly after it took place, said he found Mrs. Watson tossed out of the car.

She was said to be in "fair" condition this morning by officials at Good Samaritan Hospital in Portland. She was treated first at a Longview hospital and then moved.

Damage to the 1953 model car she was driving was set at $1,800.

Rex K. Watson was the driver of a car which went off Old Pacific Highway at Rocky Point Friday about 7:30 p.m. The auto went down a 75-foot embankment ending up on its roof on the Weyerhaeuser Timber Co. tracks. Before the car could be moved a logging train struck the vehicle. Watson was the only person in the car.

He suffered severe facial lacerations and was treated at a Longview hospital. The 1955 model car he was driving was a total loss.

Watson was charged with drunk driving in a complaint signed by Kalama Justice L. P. Brown.

The engineer of the log train which struck the car said someone had attempted to flag him down, but he didn't have time to stop his train.

Strauss Will Report To Ike On Atom Talks

FRASER, Colo. (AP) — President Eisenhower next week will get a first hand report on the Geneva atoms-for-peace conference from Lewis L. Strauss, chairman of the Atomic Energy Committee.

The President flies back East to address the American Bar Assn. Convention in Philadelphia Wednesday.

In Philadelphia Eisenhower also will meet with Seaborn Collins, national commander of the American Legion.

After the Bar Assn. speech he will fly back to Washington to pick up Mrs. Eisenhower, then take off on the return flight to Denver.

At his mountain ranch here in Fraser, the President put aside vacation activities for two hours yesterday to conduct this official

Coal Miners To Get Pay Boost

WASHINGTON (AP) — A new $2-a-day pay raise for many soft coal miners was reported ready for announcement today.

The boost, which would come in two stages, could set the pattern for the entire soft and hard coal industry.

John L. Lewis, 75-year-old president of the United Mine Workers Union, summoned his 200-man wage-policy committee for a late afternoon meeting, presumably to ratify a new coal labor pact.

The reported agreement was said to call for a 15-cents-an-hour increase, effective Sept. 1 and a further 10-cent raise to take effect next April 1.

Lewis was reported to have reached agreement privately this week with Harry M. Moses, president of the Bituminous Coal Operators Assn.

CHRISTMAS 1955

Hi Everyone,

Here I am at Brooke Army Hospital at Ft. Sam Houston in San Antonio, Texas. If I have to be incarcerated in a hospital, this, so far, appears to be the place to be... nice, warm sunshine (today it is 81°), pleasant people who speak funny, and lots and lots of *men*.

There are six buildings, each having from 300 to 600 patients. Mine has 600, with only 30 of us being women. Now I am only 20, the closet to my age is 35, married, and in an iron lung. With the remaining being men and the biggest percentage of those in their 20's, who do you think gets the most attention from the guys who are hungry, not for food, but for female camaraderie?

The flight down was NOT what one would call ordinary. I was strapped to a litter with a device much like those used on patients at Steilacoom. They were making sure I could not 'move', like that was possible. The litter was hooked to the wall of a B-52 outfitted as a hospital plane. The only other passengers from Tacoma were my brother, Dale, and an empty baby incubator. The cockpit crew kept blaring out wisecracks such as 'Look at that polar bear' and 'Mount McKinley looks great today', but I knew the difference between Mt. McKinley and Mt. Shasta. We landed in San Francisco where they deployed the incubator, and picked up a flight nurse and 30 servicemen from the war zone, all suffering from battle fatigue. They were sedated and strapped to litters. They proved to be no problem until we got into a storm with bad turbulence over Arizona. They got motion sickness and kept both the nurse and Dale hustling with the barf basins. Needless to say, they weren't fast enough at times. The pilot made an emergency landing in New Mexico where we were transported from the plane to a base hospital while the 'debris' was removed and the plane fumigated. Then the procedure was reversed and we were off once more. I'm not sure Dale would offer to escort me anywhere again.

Shortly after I arrived, my mom came to spend two weeks with me. Her room at the visitor's building was free, but her meals were not. In the end, though, the hospital did provide most of her meals.

The food here is wonderful, especially after the baby food I had in the hospital in Portland. Now that I am no longer bed-ridden, I can have solid food. Because there are so many patients in this building, and unless a patient absolutely has to have a special diet, we are all fed the same fare. Therefore, we women get the same huge amounts as these hungry, robust men. It is far more than I can eat, so mom and I share. The head cook is a true Texas chef. He offers us such fine delicacies as okra, which I had never been exposed to, and cornbread dressing, Yuk! After having cornmeal 'mush' for breakfast and fried cornmeal mush for dinner as a kid during the depression, I swore I would never eat *anything* with cornmeal in it when grown. They bring us Texas beef for just about every meal---chipped beef on toast for breakfast, roast beef sandwiches for lunch and huge beefsteaks for dinner. I don't think they know chicken or fish exist. I have had so much beef that I'm sure I'm growing horns.

I am in the rehabilitation building along with others who have polio, burns, paralysis or those who are in need of physical therapy. I go twice a day for P.T. and occupational therapy, each session being from 2-4 hours. My therapist made me a gizmo, which holds a pencil that I can use to peck out a letter on the typewriter. You are my guinea pigs so excuse the cross outs. I haven't yet mastered the ability to use the type eraser.

During therapy I met a couple of guys (both paratroopers with bad jumps, Gary in a brace from a broken neck, not paralyzed, and Ray in a leg brace using crutches because of a broken hip) who come often to my ward, drag me into a wheelchair and haul me off to the service center. This is a risky adventure on my part as this building is connected to the center via a long tunnel that goes downhill most of the way. They think it is terribly funny to let go of my chair, which then ricochets off the walls as I gain speed. It would put any carnival ride to shame. It is a wonder I stay vertical in my chair.

At the center we play cards; some play pool while others try their bodies at dancing. Gary has even tried to do a jitterbug with me plus chair. However, the under-the-leg maneuver didn't work so well. I won't go into the injury Gary sustained, but he didn't walk too well for a while.

Quite often Hollywood comes to entertain. We've had Bob Hope, Red Skelton, George and Gracie and the Glen Miller Band.

Some stars come around to the wards. Now girls, I know you are jealous. Kirk Douglas KISSED me. After inquiring as to why someone as young I was in here and listening to my replies, he turned to leave and as he did he asked, "How come they let 14-year-olds drive in Washington?" Having a baby face got the kiss, but had he known my real age, I'm sure I would have received a handshake like the other women.

It has taken me several days to peck this out so it is now a New Year's letter; therefore, I'll add my 21st birthday story.

Gary and Ray decided between them that I should celebrate it as they did theirs with some drinks. I was just settling down to sleep when a hand covered my mouth and a sinister voice said, "Don't make a sound." The next thing I knew, I was in my chair and whisked through the dark into an elevator and out of the building headed toward the closest bar, which happens to be in the Mexican section of town. Now lights go out at ten on week nights and everyone had better be there when they do bed checks. I am never checked as it would be a miracle performed by Jesus if I got out of bed. How those two got away with it they never divulged. We must have looked quite comical as we entered the bar; all of us in hospital p.j.'s, one on crutches, one in a neck brace and me in my lovely chariot. Before they could order our drinks, a fight broke out complete with screams and knives. We hightailed it out of there as fast as our broken bodies could move. Roger Bannister, move over. A safe distance away, we laughed so hard that the boys had to sit down. The next morning, I was greeted by the head nurse asking if I had fun. So much for 'sneaking'.

My parents, Dale, his wife, Phyllis, and my 22-year-old nephew, Dell, drove down from Boise, Idaho, to spend Christmas with me. Dell wanted to go see what I did in P.T. so I decided to have some fun. To exercise my muscles, they use electric shocks, which were quite painful at first, but by this time my body had adjusted to them. After I was situated and informing Dell that these were painful, I told him it would help if he would hold my hand. As he landed back on his feet after a three-foot jump, and letting out with a yell, which brought laughs from my fellow patients, he said he would never forgive me, but I know differently. He is too kind to hold a grudge.

So goes my first year of incarceration without having committed a crime.

Many thanks to all who contributed to my money tree. They had to remove the money immediately and put it in the safe. Things seem to disappear around here. Mainly our goodies. We have this 6' Italian orderly who has beautiful eyes, but that is where the beauty ends. He has a belly like a pregnant hippo, reeks of garlic and brags about everything from his great service on the battlefield to the process of cutting his toenails. We all doubt that he has ever been out of the U.S. let alone on a battlefield. Anyway, we suspect he is our culprit.

I miss you all. With hopes to see or hear from you soon, I remain your fun-loving relative and friend.

Shirley

CHRISTMAS 1956

Reflecting back on the year. Gary, Ray and I continued our forays to the service center. I also met a guy from Florida whose last name is 'Toledo'. Isn't that funny? I told him he had a town named after him, and he said, "I know." Alas he was referring to Toledo, Spain not Toledo, Wash. Adding him to our clique, he made a good 4th for our card playing, which had advanced to pinochle, spades, hearts and canasta. He entertained us with his stories about crocodiles, swamps and other aspects of living in the South, some things exaggerated I'm quite sure, but entertaining anyway. He thought it appropriate to give me his extra set of dog tags so all would know where I came from.

I did forget to tell you about my unusual, but humorous, gift I got from the construction workers I had waited on at the Shake Shop each day for over a year. It was pair of black lace panties with all of their names painted on them, with Dick's being printed conveniently in that unmentionable place.

The woman who was in the iron lung finally exited it in March, making it easier to visit with her. Her husband is a pilot who flies one of the new jet airplanes. After squeezing from him all of the details of jet flying, I told him it was something I would like to experience. Of course, regulations would never allow him to take a passenger, but it didn't stop me from harassing him about taking me. Then one Sunday, he told me he was going to take me for a ride around the city, saying that I couldn't leave without seeing where I had been. He did do that, and then drove to the airfield to show me where he worked. The next thing I knew, his buddy put all kinds of garb on me, they threw me into their plane, and off we went. I hope you can picture me screaming with no sound emerging, my lips turning inside out, my ears clinging to my head tightly, my lungs bursting and my eyes leaving their sockets. Through my earphones, he was telling me what we were flying over, but who could see? Thirty minutes later, we were back on the ground having flown as far as Kentucky and back. I wanted to get down and kiss the ground, but since that was impossible, I just grabbed the nearest thing to it, a pole. While splitting their guts laughing, he and his conspirator made me promise never to tell anyone in authority about my 'ride' for it was definitely a violation of their command. It was a journey I shall never forget.

In August, Ray was released to go home for 30 days before returning to duty. Toledo was next in September and Gary in October. Others I had met filled the void, but it just was not the same. Then in Nov., I flew out again in a hospital plane dropping off others in Denver, Great Falls, Montana, Salt Lake City, and finally me at McChord Air Force Base, in Tacoma, Washington, where I was kept at the base hospital for five days in order to discharge me to my family. On Sunday, they fed me their usual lunch of cold cuts, cheese, etc. Later, I realized why military men complain of the food. Talk about flu. It doesn't compare with the gut wrenching cramps I was experiencing. Since my stomach muscles are paralyzed, I cannot throw up, making it impossible to get relief. And who should show up but Toledo, Washington friends I hadn't seen for over a year. Needless to say, they cut their visit short and scampered out of there.

I'm home, in Toledo, Wash., reluctantly. It was hard to leave a place where I had lived for almost a year as I was with similar people and staff who understood me and my limitations. I have met some special friends with whom I have shared laughs and tears. However, I must get used to this new life back among the able-bodied.

It is going to be great to spend Christmas at home. Many friends have dropped by, one of those being Gary*, as he lives in Longview, Wash., 30 miles from me. Those three guys will always remain friends if only through letters. We have so much to do in rebuilding our lives, though mine is quite limited.

I have to laugh at comments from others such as 'You actually look normal', and the best, 'I thought you were paralyzed.' I have scary visions of what they thought I would look like.

May you all have a Merry Christmas and love to all,

Shirley

*Gary lost his life a few years after returning home. The boat he and some friends were in capsized while going across the Columbia River Bar. Gary's body was never recovered.

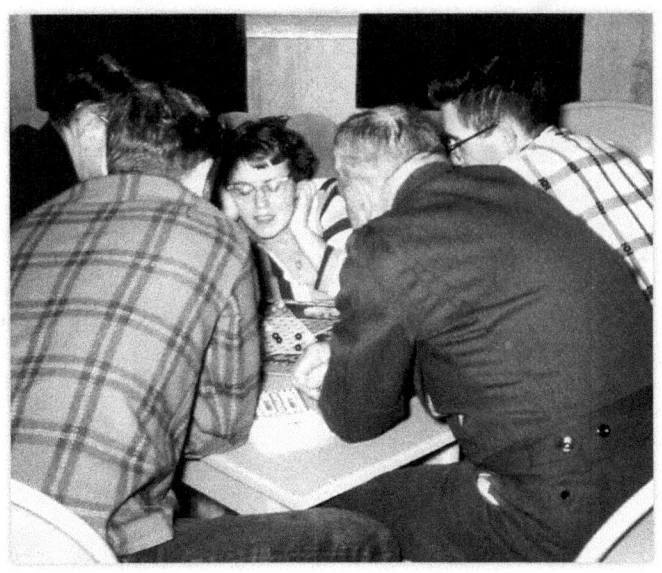

At home for Christmas, playing board games with Dad and the brothers...

My Parents & Siblings

Back Row, Left to Right (standing in order from youngest to oldest): Joseph 'Bert' (Kathy, Fran), Atherton 'Addy' Warren (Claylene, June, Verna), Daniel 'Dan' V. (Vivian), Henry 'Dale' (Phyllis), Herschell Francis (Beth), Keith Gill (Marilyn, Helen), John William 'Bill' (Mary), Thomas 'Ross' (Hattie), Melna 'Millie' (Jake) Nelson, Anna Gwenlion 'Gwen' (Jim) Packer, Walter 'Leland' (Naomi)

Front Row, Left to Right: Mother Anna Elizabeth (Gill) Stinger, Me, Father John Walter

CHRISTMAS 1957

Being as my parents are old enough to be my grandparents, they just could not care for me. My brothers decided they and their wives would be my salvation. Therefore, I found myself back in the city that I was born in, Pocatello, Idaho, living with Bill and Mary who have five children from Janet age 15 to Terry 1.5.

Winter passed, and the first spring day, I had Mary wheel me out into the sun to warm my body thoroughly. I have poor circulation so I never seem to get warm. I laid on my chaise lounge reading for several hours. Big mistake! The next morning, I woke to my lips so badly swollen from fever blisters that I could hardly open my mouth. I couldn't even hold a straw between them, resulting in Mary having to feed me for several days by pouring soup through a funnel. The kids said I looked like one of the African natives that stretch their lips. Not funny.

Summer came, finding me outside again on a chaise lounge reading while soaking up some sun after a long snowy, windy winter. That night as Mary was undressing me, she found a sand spider crushed between my thigh and jeans. It had apparently been crawling up my leg when I had a muscle spasm eliminating it from existence. Bill immediately got a flashlight to go find its mate as they "marry" for life. "Why did he care?" you ask. Sand spiders are not only very ugly, they are extremely poisonous, causing death if one is not treated right away. Had that bugger succeeded in traveling on his path up my leg, I would not be writing this letter.

Bill, Mary, Janet, Peggy,
Bill, Rick, Terry

Janet informed Mary that she was in need of sanitary napkins. Since Mary wasn't going into town that day, she asked Bill to pick some up for her. The next morning as Janet was in the bathroom getting ready for school, we heard her yell. Mary, thinking something drastic was happening to Janet, hurried to her rescue but came back chuckling. Bill had bought napkins with flowers, and since they were new on the market, Janet had never seen nor heard of them. Quite the unassuming devil, my brother.

Another day, Janet came into the living room in her skivvies and bra to tell me something. Her dad, thinking she should be more fully clothed, looked toward the screened door and remarked, "Come on in, Wolf." Wolf is the neighbor boy Janet has a slight crush on. I doubt she had ever gotten dressed that fast.

Hooker? In my wildest dreams I never thought I would become one, but 'hooker' I did become. Having lived on my own and working since age 13, this life I had been thrust into had become quite boring. Get up, read to Terry, play cards with one of the other kids if I could rope them into it, or just watch television. Finally, my local therapist took pity and designed a gadget by which I could hook rugs. So a hooker was born. Mary would draw a design on burlap, and I'd spend a few hours each day hooking. Many friends and relatives were pressed upon to accept my crude pieces of art. I am not known for any artistic talent, and more than likely, will never develop it. All I can draw are flies and that is only in the summer!

On New Year's Eve, the kids begged to stay up and watch the new year in on the T.V. After some discussion as to whether they could stay awake that long, the parents agreed. All four older kids made it with the exception of Peggie, age 13. The next morning the other kids were razzing her about falling asleep, which she denied emphatically saying, "My eyes might have been asleep, but my ears weren't!"

A few nights ago, I dreamed the doctors gave me a spinal transplant. The donor of the spinal cord was a cow. All went well. I was normal once more. However, when I tried walking, I heard a clomp, clomp, clomp. I looked down only to find, in place of human feet, I had 'hooves'.

Out of stories. I'm looking out at three feet of snow, wishing instead that I were there in your three inches of rain.

Happy days ahead to all.

Love,

Shirley

Sitting on my chaise with niece and nephew

CHRISTMAS 1958

Dear Toledoans, etc.

I'm still in Pocatello at Bill and Mary's. Each morning while the oldest four of Bill's kids are getting ready for school, I entertain Terry who likes to sit on my back (I sleep on my stomach), where I bounce him up and down. However, one morning, I was lying on my back, and Terry not knowing the difference, sat on my face. All of a sudden, something was trickling down my chin. There were no plastic pants on that kid and he had no sense of where or when he should pee. I was trying to yell for Mary to come get him, but the more I yelled, the more pee ran into my mouth. I've heard lost people drink their urine to keep alive, but I don't think I was lost, just incapable of defending myself against an invader.

My nephew, Dell, lives in Pocatello also. For those of you who don't already know, I have four nieces and nephews older than me, Dell being one of them. He has become my buddy. We go for rides to the outdoor theater and he will even baby-sit me if both Bill and Mary have to be gone. He is to blame for my first nightmare. He had insisted I go see a 'great' movie that had just come to the theater. It was my debut to horror movies, "Psycho," this one where the female visitor is murdered while taking a shower. I refuse to ever shower at a hotel/motel again.

Dell was also the cause of my first wheelchair spill. He wanted me to see a gopher digging his tunnel through Bill's front yard. Interesting and educational. As he was 'racing' me back toward the house, my front wheel caught in a rut and out I went, face plastered into the muddy dirt. More education. I learned thereafter to hang on by wrapping my arm around the push handle of the chair.

In August, I went to spend a few weeks with my brother, Herschell, and his wife, Beth. They live about ten miles away. The fold-out couch was my bed and it was there that Beth had stripped off my night clothes just as the doorbell rang. Without thinking that I was lying there in the buff, she invited in two repairmen who had come to fix her phone. "I think we had better come back later," one said. Not knowing that I was incapable of grabbing something to cover my exposed bod, one can only imagine what they surmised they had almost gotten themselves roped into. I made sure I was not present when they came back.

Since I know you are having a good laugh, I shall say good-bye for this year.

God bless

Love, Shirley

P.S. I know it is not kosher to type a signature, BUT try writing holding a pen grasped in your teeth and a paper wiggling back and forth between two unworkable hands with the result looking like what a trained monkey might write; then you'll know why I type my John Hancock.

CHRISTMAS 1959

After two years at Bill's, I am now with Dale and Phyllis in Boise, Idaho. Mary was expecting a baby so was not able to tug me around. This brother has two small children, Rhonda and Carol. After being there for a couple of days, I heard giggling outside the window that I was sitting near. I looked up from my book just in time to hear Rhonda saying to several of her little friends, "See, there is my 'crooked' aunt." Obviously she didn't remember the word crippled.

Rhonda was missing. She had been playing in the yard in her sandbox where I could see her from the window to check on her as I was reading. All of a sudden, she wasn't there. Phyllis checked around the back of the house, hoping Rhonda had wandered back there. No Rhonda. Phyllis then checked with the neighbors, but no one had seen that little girl. Phyllis called the police, and then she and neighbors began scouting the area, but she was nowhere to be found. Then the police called. Fearing the worst, I then heard Phyllis saying, "Thank God." A man had made some deliveries in the area. Rhonda had spied the back door of his car open, climbed in, laid on the floor and fallen asleep. The man had made several other stops before he had to get something from his back seat and was shocked to find this child. He had no idea who she was or when she had entered his vehicle. Not knowing what else to do, he took her to the police station. After that, one of us stayed outside with her during playing time.

Summers I've been spending back in Toledo with friends, Rose and Son, as Idaho summers are just too hot for me. After going shopping with Rose and her mom one day, they were carrying me from the pickup to the house, Rose with her arms under mine and Lucille's under my knees. By the time we got to the house, Rose had barely a hold on me and Lucille's had slipped to my ankles causing my fanny to drag on the ground. As Rose had to go potty, we were laughing hysterically Needless to say, she never made it to the right room.

Now I am in Longview living with Keith and Marilyn. I swear I have nothing to do with fertility, but Phyllis also got pregnant. Marilyn wants a baby; maybe I'll bring her luck.

It is quiet and rainy and no new stories.

Happy, happy holidays,

Love from ME

CHRISTMAS 1960

Christmas 1960

Last December, I came to Longview, Washington, to live with brother, Keith, and wife, Marilyn.

Living in a 10-foot-wide mobile home at Keith's proved to be a challenge for Marilyn and me. After getting me dressed each morning after Keith had left for work, it took some ingenuity to get me into the living room. Mobile homes are well known for narrow doors, thus neither a wheelchair, nor the chaise lounge that I usually spend my day on, would fit through the opening. Between the two of us, we finally figured out she could pull the bed down across the door opening, scoot me to the bottom, pull the chaise to the opening on the other side and drag me onto the chaise. This worked fine until one morning the chaise decided it didn't like to be there and slid away just as Marilyn was dragging me onto it. There I was with my head on the bed, my feet on the chaise and my butt on the floor. Tears were flowing from laughing, leaving Marilyn incapable of getting me up. I convinced her to go next door and get Doris to help. From then on she made sure she put a block behind the wheels of the chaise before the BIG transfer.

In order for my muscles not to get stiff, my brothers once a day help me with exercises; bend the legs and push, lift the legs straight up, and then help me with sit-ups. After one such session, I was sweating profusely that continued on through the night. While still in the Texas hospital, I had discovered that when I sweat, it is an indication that I am hurting somewhere. It is then an exercise in exploration to find where the pain is centralized. It was no contest this time, though. When Marilyn was getting me dressed, she discovered that I was black and blue from my thigh to my big toe. Apparently, Keith didn't know his own strength and had pushed my leg beyond its kicking point.

My brother, Bill, works for the railroad, granting him free passes for him and his family. When they came to visit, we chose to pick them up in Portland, saving them the trouble of changing trains to come on north. We were running late, hurrying across the tracks, and then the next moment I went flying out of my chair face first into the cinders. The wheel on my wheelchair had caught on one of the rails, tipping my chair forward. No damage to me but for a bruised ego.

Marilyn had some errands to run, but didn't want to leave me alone, and I didn't want to go with her. I assured her I would be all right while reading and lounging in the sun on my chaise lounge. She hadn't been gone long when the neighbor's dog came by, jumped up on me, and while I was trying to evict him, I heard a crackling sound. The lounge broke in half leaving me AND the dog, who was still resting on my chest, with lounge pad and my keister on the cement patio. I really had not planned on spending the afternoon in a hammock, but that seemed to be my destination until Marilyn got back. However, Doris missed her dog, came looking for her, and with help got me back upright in my w/c (wheelchair). I doubt Mare will let me talk her into leaving me at home by myself again.

So on with the festivities, I remain your source of amusement for another year.

Have a great holiday.

Love, Shirley

CHRISTMAS 1962

Greetings,

I'm back with Bill and Mary who now have added Calvin, now 5, making them a family of eight.

In January, to give them a rest from me and me from them, I went to spend a few weeks with Dick and Delores in Idaho Falls, Idaho. They had moved there after Dick graduated from college where he found a job at Arco, a nuclear plant out in the sagebrush plain. While there, I got my first chest cold post trauma. I sneeze like a cat, and tragically, I cough the same way. This, however, does not provide enough air to get rid of the gunk that has taken up residence in my lungs. To help me do so, innovative Dick decided he could be my chest power by pushing on my diaphragm.* Success! Up came the invaders. Billy and Linda just could not understand why 'Aunt' Shirley could no longer spend her day reading and playing card games with them as each time I tried to talk, it would bring on another spasm of coughs and Delores running to push. I am sure they were relieved to see me off to Pocatello once again.

Mary was canning beets, and to be smart, I told her I would help her, knowing there was no way this ole cripple could peel and cut beets. However, the next thing I knew, she had plunked down a pan of those darn red veggies in front of me, put a towel tucked into my shirt and promptly told me to rub the peelings off. After several tries, I found the only way to remove the ends was to bite them off. Not sanitary! I knew the pressure cooker would kill any germs I might leave behind. When done, I looked like I had been in the worst fight of my life. My face was blood red, my hands were blood red, let alone the towel, but the critters were peeled and ready to slice. Thanks be that she didn't trust me with a knife.

One evening, Mary had cooked up a nice dinner. I cannot remember what it was, but Rick took a huge helping. "You will not be able to eat all of that," his mother remarked. He insisted that he could, but sure enough, he couldn't. The rule of the house was if she filled their plates, and they couldn't eat it all, fine, but if you helped yourself you had to eat it all. Everyone finished eating, table was cleared, dishes were done, but Rick was still sitting in front of his half-eaten food. We all had gone to the living room when we heard a gagging noise. Rick had upchucked. Mary figured he had learned his lesson after he also had to clean it up and hightail himself off to bed.

Not much going on with me, no spills, no spiders crawling up my legs, so will close my diatribe for this year.

Merry Christmas.

Love to all, Shirley

*When retyping this much later in the next century, I realized, Dick had invented the Heimlich Method before it was published by Dr. Heimlich.

CHRISTMAS 1963

Dear Friends,

I am back in Boise, where I spent most of the time this last year going to my parents' home from my brother, Dale's, to visit with them each day as my mother was not well. In August, she had a stroke, which kept her bedridden. In late October, she had another one, and she passed away on November 5th. No matter how hard her life was, Mom was always cheerful, and her singing greeted us each day upon our return from school. She often grabbed one of us and danced around our large kitchen. She is responsible for all of us loving music, playing instruments and dancing. Having raised 12 children, it is amazing how she managed to be so light hearted. She was vital to our well-being and shall be missed by all.

Dad & Mother, 1958

One of Mom's greatest wishes came true. She lived to see Keith and Marilyn get a baby, Barbie, whom they adopted in the early fall. Honestly, I had nothing to do with it.

To give Dale and Phyllis a break and while she had a month off from her job as a school secretary, I went to Denver, Colorado, to spend two weeks with my sister Gwen, her husband, Jim, and their two children, Bonnie and Brent. One evening, I was telling them about a paraplegic friend of mine who had an apartment, which in order to enter, he had to negotiate his chair up eight steps. He chose this particular one to keep strength in his arms, build muscles, and big muscles he did have. He would put Charles Atlas to shame. He would do a quick wheelie, which would bounce him up one step, balance there, then do another. Brent, who is 16, was listening and seemed transfixed. The next day, while I was lounging and visiting with Gwen on the patio, we heard an awful crashing sound and a piercing scream. Brent was lying at the foot of the basement stairs, my wheelchair on top of him and moaning. As it turned out, he was trying to duplicate my friend's stair climbing, but instead of starting at the bottom, he had decided that going down would be easier. No damage to chair and no damage to kid but for a few bruises.

Dale and Phyllis have great neighbors, Ivan and Jean Andrus and Lavar and Betty Thomas. Jean and Betty, to get me out of the house, often take me for strolls around the neighborhood. After one walk on a fairly hot day, they decided to get me into Betty's house for some cool refreshments. This meant they would have to get me and my chair up a flight of six cement steps. With Jean in back pulling and Betty in front pushing, up we went. All of a sudden as we got to the last step, I found myself heading back down with Jean under my chair cushioning my head. No bumps or bruises for me, but poor Jean's legs suffered scraped and bloodied shins. Needless to say, we cancelled the libations.

Dale and Phyllis had taken the kids to a church program. I wasn't feeling well, so I elected to stay home. I got to feeling worse and wanted to lie down. I called Lavar and asked him if he would come lay me on my bed. His comment, "Sure, I'll 'lay' you on the bed, and I'll also bring some wine." I had to restate my request!

My brothers here in Boise have ski boats. With two large lakes in the hills, they look forward to the first warm day to go skiing.

Not sure if I wanted to ride in the hot car the ten miles to the lake, I was protesting going along. Dale promised me that I would be cool enough, and before I knew it, I was seated in the boat 'behind' the car and screeching as he drove off. However, he did stop after a few blocks and transferred me to the car. After all, he didn't want to explain to a trooper about the screaming lunatic he was transporting.

After church one lovely Sunday, Dale was pushing me home, which was about three blocks, two of them downhill. He said he needed some exercise. He was running, with me hanging on with both arms hooked behind the chair's handles, a trick I'd learned after being dumped out several other times. All of a sudden, a wheel was rolling down the hill in front of me, and I was lying on my side, BUT I was still in my chair. He uprighted me and continued on traveling with me in the chair with only one wheel, picking the other wheel up on the way. He wouldn't admit it, but I'm sure that was a bigger workout than he planned.

While Dale was helping me with my exercises, Carol was bugging me to read to her. As she wasn't paying any attention to her dad when he said "not now," he finally got exasperated and told her to "go take a powder". A few minutes later, she returned covered from head to toe in bath powder. After all, that is what her dad told her to do. With that I shall sign off for this year.

God bless, Merry Christmas and Happy New Year.

Love,

Shirley

Phyllis, David, Dale, Carol

CHRISTMAS 1964

Hello from Boise,

I am back at Dale's after spending part of the summer with Rose and Son and part with the Brenemans.

On the way taking me to Toledo and my dad along for the ride, Dale went to pass a gasoline truck/tanker when the truck, without signaling, turned left in front of us. Dale skidded to a stop, but he still slid into the tanker throwing me onto the floor from the back seat where I was riding. No injuries were sustained by either me, my dad, or Dale, unless you count the prickly rose bush and the watermelon from his garden that Dad was taking to Rose, both of which flew from back of the seat and landed on my head and body, the melon splitting open and causing juice to dye my white shirt a nice color of light red and the bush thorns inflicting a few scratches. Because they were taking precautions in case of a gas leak causing a fire, they got me out and laid me on the nice soft grass. It took some lengthy explanations to convince onlookers that I was not covered in blood but with sticky, sweet watermelon juice. I'm sure they were perplexed when I didn't arise and chat with them. A bent fender pulled away from the tire, and a filled-out accident report completed, we were once again on our way.

In the fall, it was off to the Breneman's in Richland, Washington, where Diane, age 3, and Marc, age 4, entertained me with their antics. They were constantly getting into trouble. 1. Diane came into the house looking rather strange as she had big lumps in her unders. Since she had been potty trained from age two, Delores couldn't believe she had had a "poopy" accident. Upon inspection,

Delores found several potatoes. 2. They both were put down for a nap. Usually, they never settled down to sleep without Delores having to threaten them by carrying in the dreaded belt (She said she had only lightly used it once, but keeping it hanging on the fridge handle circumvented all other spankings), but this day, they were exceptionally quiet. Deciding to check, she found them doing nothing, unless you count the windows now devoid of curtains and dresser drawers empty of clothing. 3. They enjoyed emptying the charcoal grill of its briquettes and coloring each other black. 4. Using four letter words the neighbor boys delighted in teaching them always got them in trouble with their mom.

Dick and son, Billy, had gone fishing, returning with two large, ugly catfish, both still alive. Having never seen one of these creatures, I was asking some questions, one of which was how they would kill them since being out of water didn't seem to be causing them to expire. Dick explained, as he headed for the kitchen, that he would have to hit them in the head with a hammer. Soon, I heard a loud bam, bam, bam that seemed to go on endlessly. Being squeamish, I decided right then that if they were that hard to kill, I was not eating the poor things. And I didn't. Later, Delores said they were all forcing themselves not to laugh as Dick was merely hitting the hammer on the breadboard, not the fish.

My stay at the Breneman's was cut short as I started swelling and was in pain. We all thought it best to return to Boise to see a doctor. The diagnosis was large bladder stones cutting off the urine flow, which was backing up into my system. On to the operating room. A local anesthesia, a mirror hanging over me, and I was soon devoid of the stones while watching the procedure in reflection. Not something I would want to watch on someone else, but it was interesting to see and hear what goes on in that room.

There is nothing else of laughable interest to report, so will wish you all good thoughts and Happy Holidays.

Love to all, Shirley

CHRISTMAS 1965

Greetings from Boise,

I'm still at brother Dale's. I try and go visit my dad a couple of times a week. He had a slight stroke a while back, but has recovered well enough to go back to working in his vegetable and flower gardens. He loves his roses and grows a big enough garden to feed a family of ten. My bothers' families that live here make good use of it. As Dad was used to my mother's homemade bread, he refused to eat bakery bread. His philosophy was, "No wonder they call it Wonder Bread. You eat 10 slices and wonder if you've had anything to eat." Therefore, he decided he would make his own bread. I happened to be there on the day of his first attempt. He insisted he make me a sandwich from his work of art. Now how do you tell your adoring father that his creation was anything but edible? I managed to choke down a few bites before he tried it himself. His only comment was, "It doesn't quite taste like your mother's." After that, he let my sister-in-law, Hattie, make his bread.

While downtown shopping in the spring, I had Keith, age 4, on my lap while Phyllis pushed me down the street. The front wheel caught on a crack, chair flipped, and out I went, landing on top of Keith. Expecting the poor kid to be cut, bleeding or smothered, he shocked us as he crawled out from under me laughing, and asked his mother to do that again. With help from a passing gentleman, she got me back into the chair, but Keith did not get another free ride that day.

We were having a family get-together at Dale's one day, when they noticed Carol, six, was missing. After searching the house, they turned to checking the neighborhood as well. They were about to call the police when she came out of the bedroom. She had gotten sleepy, had crawled into one of the sleeping bags piled in the corner by overnight guests, and conked out. Being the second of his kids to "disappear," one wonders which one will be next.

In the fall, I spent my usual few weeks in Richland, Washington, with Dick and Delores. It was time for parent conferences, and they were worried about what the nun would have to tell them about their five-year-old, Marc, known for his salty language that the neighbor kids had taught him, plus his penchant for being mischievous. When they came back from their visit, I asked how it went. Laughing, Delores said, "The Sister expounded on Marc's exemplary behavior and said if all of her students were like him, she would not have any problems." Marc was summoned from the basement, where as usual, he wasn't being the best kid on the block. Delores asked, "Why are you so naughty at home and so good at school?" With the face of innocence, he replied, "Cause you're not a witch."

Nothing else exciting to write about so will close.

Have a great NEW YEAR.

Love, Crip ..... as the kids have decided my name should be.

CHRISTMAS 1966

I am back at Keith's and Marilyn's. Since I was last here, they have adopted another little girl, Steffanie, six months. Barbie, being three and having had all of her parents' attention plus then having to share with Steffanie, really disliked me intruding more into her life. Whenever Marilyn had to pay any attention to me, she would stand around the corner and yell. "Git Auntie." Every time, it would crack Mare and me up. She has gotten past that now and insists on sitting across from me to eat off my plate, and she loves to ride on my lap. A few times she has brought my w/c out and wants to go to town. That is about the only time I use it. The chaise is better as I can lie down whenever my 'butt' starts complaining.

Steffanie is now one and the most determined child I have met. She is so cute but a challenge. She'll reach for something she shouldn't have, Mare will say "no," but she'll keep on reaching. Next step, a little swat on the hands, but still she will keep reaching. With such determination, Steffanie should go far in life.

To give Marilyn a break, I went to Rose and Son's in late March. The morning of April 1st, and Shirley's (their daughter, named for me) 5th birthday, she came from her bedroom dressed, but not in her usual play clothes. "Shirley, why are you dressed in your good clothes?" Rose inquired. "You said when I turned five, I could go to school," she replied. It took quite a bit of explaining to get her to understand she had to wait until school started in the fall.

In August I again went to spend a week at Rose's. On a hot day, she was burning some trash, which sent a spark onto the dry

Leland & Naomi

grass of the field behind the house. Since the fire trucks run with volunteer firemen, it took some time to round up men to travel the five miles to douse the fire. After a chastising from the men, she was able to slink back into the house. As I was on my chaise, all I could do was pray they got it out before it spread to the house, and I'd end up charcoal.

My oldest brother, Leland, and his wife, Naomi, came to visit. I had been doing some background on my parents and my siblings. Some dates just didn't make sense. Leland and Naomi's wedding date and the birth of their first child, Arnold (both in 1930) didn't match up. According to my records, the dates showed Arnold was born six months post wedding. While they were visiting, I decided to get it straightened out so I asked them which date was incorrect, wedding or birth. "They are right," Leland said. "No, they aren't," Naomi argued. This went back and forth for a bit when Leland exclaimed, "Naomi, do you think kids these days invented sex before marriage?" End of discussion.

May your holiday bring you many gifts of love.

Shirley

CHRISTMAS 1967

Greetings from the college girl,

Yeah! Relief from boredom. In April, my doctor had recommended to a young man from DVR (Dept. of Vocational Rehabilitation) to visit me to see if he thought I could get some training for a job so that I could support myself. Daniel, the DVR man, after talking with me for quite some time suggested I see a psychologist to determine if I was a candidate for college. She gave me several psych tests, grilled me about my desires and capabilities, and decided my brain was considered intact and functioning. She didn't stress how well, however. She then suggested to both Daniel and I that I needed some vocational rehabilitation to build up wheelchair tolerance.

With funds from DVR, I was off to Good Samaritan Rehab Center in Puyallup, Washington. It is a small unit with only ten patients but with three times the number of staff as patients. This was how my day went:

1. Up at six.

2. Bundled in a towel and carried to the bath tub by Paul. No thrill there since he is 50ish.

3. A quick scrubbing by an aide.

4. Reverse by Paul.

5. Dressed, teeth brushed, hair combed and a little make-up applied.

6. Breakfast in a little dining area.

7. Eight o'clock we ten are in group exercises with P.T., Mary Louise. Swing those arms, stretch and twist the necks and heads, keep it up until you wish you were dead, pull weights from wall (I had leather, mitten-like devices they strapped to the bars since I can't grasp) and breathe, breathe. Then using the same mittens, I had to lift small barbells, which became bigger ones until I was lifting 35 lb. Anyone want to arm wrestle?

8. Lunch and an hour's rest. I take my rest on the roof where I can read and enjoy the sun.

9. At two, we repeat the exercise routine.

10. Dinner at five then free for evening. Four of us play pinochle, hearts, and canasta or work on a jigsaw puzzle until bedtime at nine.

We could sit with whomever we wanted during meals. I sat with Fred who has brain damage. He was an engineer working on a tunnel when part of it caved in on him. He tries to talk, but his words are garbled beyond understanding plus he drools and spits. I sit with him as no one else will. Most evenings, his wife joins us. By the time I left three months later, he was improving enough so that I could understand some of his words. I heard from his wife last month. They are in Arizona. He has had his shunt removed and is making great strides, she reports.

Weekends, we were free from our grueling torture. Each Saturday for a while, a brace man visited me to fit me with a newly devised orthotic hand brace called a tenodesis splint. This has enabled me to write (no more chewing up pens and pencils trying to write while holding them between my teeth), brush my own teeth, eat, and pick up just about anything that weighs less than a lb. Linda, a children's P.T., took me out to several movies and to her house for dinners. This was a nice break from institutional fare, which actually was not that bad.

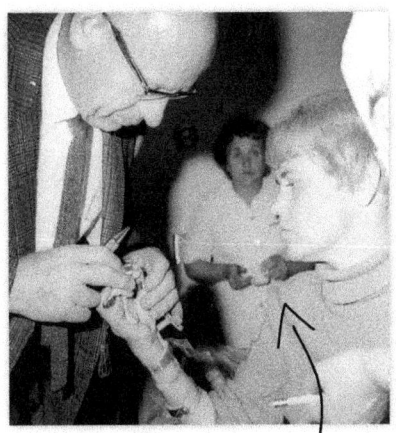

Being fitted for my hand splint

No more writing with a pencil between my teeth!

In September and back with Keith and Marilyn, I started school at Lower Columbia Junior College here in Longview. I was so scared. No one had ever attended this particular college in a wheelchair so I had no idea what to expect. Marilyn got me out of the car, into my chair, and said goodbye. My first class, English Composition, was up a flight of stairs, no elevator. With a quivering voice I asked a couple of healthy young men if they could haul me up. "Sure, it will be good weight training for basketball," they replied. Each morning after that, they met me there until my instructor realized how I was getting to her class and arranged with a downstairs history teacher to exchange classrooms. Also, another classmate observed Marilyn dragging me from the car to chair, offered to pick me up and deposit me in w/c and then pushed me to class. LCC staff bent over backwards to accommodate by also asking classmates to push me to my next class.

After being out of school for twelve years, it is difficult trying to keep up with all of these kids freshly out of high school. This became apparent in my chemistry class. Me, who never had chemistry in high school, find myself in a class with kids with 2-3 years already behind them. This is where I met Margie who was in the same predicament. Mr. Livermore referred to us as his

"The Student"

office girls as we practically lived there. I was appalled when I got an 'F' on my first test. I had never received an 'F' in my life, but as he was going over the test the next day, I found one he had marked wrong that was actually correct. I brought this to his attention, and with great aplomb, he put F+ on my paper. This from a man who has hair growing on his palm. His abnormality was a great subject of curiosity among us students. I decided since I was not exactly normal myself, I could just ask him about it. His explanation, which he chuckled through, was that he had run his hand through a paper press while working at a mill during his college years "Where do you suppose they got the skin to graft onto my hand?" he asked. I was not about to answer after all kinds of visions were running through my mind. "My hairy thigh." he replied. Puzzle solved.

This quarter didn't end very well. During finals, I got word from the nursing home that my father had passed away. I shall miss him terribly as each day after my classes, I would go to see him and read him the newspaper. As long as I could remember, Dad read the paper every day after dinner. Many of those evenings, he would fall asleep doing so. Once when I was a kid, my niece, Dell, and I took the opportunity to sneak and polish his nails bright red. We heard him the next morning, saying " What the hell", and asking Mom for the polish remover which of course she couldn't find as we had it in bed with us. He had to go to work at the railroad yards with lovely nails. I can imagine the heckling he got from his fellow workers. We had to cough up the remover that night, but no punishment was rendered.

This has been a very long letter so must wish all goodnight and HAPPY HOLIDAYS.

Lovingly,

THE STUDENT

Shirley Watson triumphs

By Adele Ferguson
Bremerton Sun Political Affairs Columnist

OLYMPIA — Shirley Watson of Toledo (in Lewis County) is a quadriplegic, the result of an auto accident.

She is a working quadriplegic, though, and is in her second year as a remedial reading teacher at Toledo High School.

She is paid $746.33 a month, out of which she nets $548.46. Her largest expense is the $220 she pays to a full-time attendant-housekeeper at her home. She also pays $115 for rent. That leaves her $213 for utilities, food, car and medical expenses, the latter running about $50 a month.

She's single so that's all the income she has and she has to borrow to meet the bare necessities.

She couldn't figure out why she couldn't claim on her income tax what she pays in wages to her attendant.

"I cannot understand why a husband and wife who both work can claim what they pay for a babysitter (especially when it is not necessary for both to work) and I cannot claim necessary attendant care," she said.

The Internal Revenue Service informed her "if I had a husband who was the wage earner and he had to hire attendant care for me he would claim this cost on his return, but because I am the wage earner I cannot."

She doesn't mind paying a fair share to support the government, she said. "But I do mind when I feel the laws as they are stated are unfair."

Miss Watson took the matter up with U.S. Sens. Henry M. Jackson and Warren G. Magnuson and Congressman Don Bonker.

This is a problem that faces other handicapped persons besides her, who try to be self-sufficient but who would be better off if they just went on public assistance, she said.

"Not only am I (and many others) supporting myself but also providing employment for another person (my attendant) who would also be covered by public assistance," she said.

Jackson's office contacted District IRS director Michael Sassi in Seattle whose reply was that there were no statutory provisions for a tax deduction for the expense incurred. Sassi's letter was sent to her as "self-explanatory."

Bonker's office wrote Charles T. Deliee, chief of the Technical Services branch of IRS, who replied that there were no special deductions or allowances available for attendant-housekeepers employed by handicapped individuals. If their services were performed by a nurse they would be deductible but to include attendant care would require a change in the law.

Bonker wrote Miss Watson he would pursue it further. She didn't hear for a long time so she turned next to her legislator, Rep. Hugh Kalich of Toledo.

He was just starting to try to do something for her when word came from Bonker that a special ruling had been made by the IRS allowing Miss Watson to deduct both her attendant's wages and board and room.

That takes care of her, for which she's happy, but it still leaves unsolved the problem of all other persons like her, and the matter, said Kalich, shouldn't be dropped by Congress just because it disposed of this particular case.

CHRISTMAS 1968

Merry Christmas from the Semi-Learned,

A year and a quarter are now behind me. Just eight more quarters to go. After a couple of months into the year, I am back into the routine.

My favorite class this year, so far, is World History. A very diverse class it is. It is taught by a professor from India who speaks English with a thick accent, plus we have five young men from Iran and a Japanese boy. These boys amaze me. They listen to the lecture, but take their notes in Arabic and Japanese then do their hand-in lessons in English. One of our assignments was to speak in front of the class about where we were from, where we had traveled, and about our customs. I learned from the Iranians that women DO NOT get educated after they turn twelve as then they are considered marriage material. When I was twelve, I don't think I knew what sex was, nor was I even thinking about men per se. (How is that for a little/big word? See, college is teaching me something.) Also the men can have as many wives as they want, providing they can financially support them. One student asked if the women could refuse to marry. Answer "No." Can they get a divorce? Ans. "Women, no, but men can by simply saying "I divorce you,' three times." These remarks caused all the male students to say they wanted to move to Iran.

A fun class is Introduction to Psychology. Our teacher wanted us not only to know of the doo hickeys (his word, not mine) psychs use to test with but also how to use them. We used the Rorschach (ink spots), blocks that had to be assembled in a certain pattern within an assigned amount of minutes and others. However my favorite was the Galvanic Skin Response, a lie detector test. With the GSR, if you are lying, you tend to emit a little sweat on your skin, and the tester can tell you are not telling the truth. The class was in hysterics when he hooked up one student, asked him some general questions, then asked more specific ones, such as, "Do you have a girlfriend? Did you go out with her last night?" No needle flying around, but when he asked, "Did you score with her," and he answered "No" that old needle jumped around like a grasshopper dancing on a hot coal. I asked him to do mine, but when he asked some embarrassing questions with me lying like some criminals do, the needle just lay there and died. Little did he know my paralysis keeps me from sweating anywhere that I have no sense of feeling. Being a quad has some advantages. Maybe I should go into a life of crime. I could use some cash.

Spring vacation, Marilyn and I went to Portland, Oregon, to spend two days with her sister who is also a pal I grew up with... Barbara. I needed to get a few things for school. Off we went to the mall. I was in my pushchair, Barb pushing at a running pace. Thinking she would get a free ride, she hopped onto the back. Yow, over I went...backwards, ripping open Barb's new wool pants and banging my head.

Later that day, I was resting in the bedroom while Barb was fixing dinner. She had put a pan of grease on the stove to make French fries. Being distracted by her children's antics in another room, she forgot the grease. I smelled smoke and yelled. She and Marilyn ran to the kitchen only to see flames shooting toward the ceiling. Marilyn, worried that I'd be caught in a burning house, ran in and Charles Atlas style picked me up and ran out into the rain. How she held me long enough for Barb to say, "All is clear!" is beyond me. Drenched, I was once more deposited. Damage, just a very smoked-up house. The insurance rep came to appraise the damage and announced that a good coat of paint throughout the house would alleviate the problem. I don't recommend that you burn grease to get a face-lift for your walls.

Remember Fred, the brain damaged patient I made friends with in rehab? I got a letter from him thanking me for being kind during that time. He stated he understood everything then, just couldn't verbalize. He is fine now and back on an engineering job. So if I have a stroke and can't talk, watch out how you treat me. I may come back to make your life unbearable.

Must go hit the books. Just one more week until break.

Love, Shirley, the college object of curiosity

Having lunch with the girls

Our little shack

970-35   910 SOUTH RUBY   ELLENSBURG, WASHINGTON

My car

CHRISTMAS 1969

Hi Everyone,

I'm now through at LCC and ready to move on to two more years of cramming my brain with some useful and some-not-so useful info. I have a 3.8 GPA, and, yes, I am bragging. Going back to school after 12 years plus being in a w/c hasn't been easy but will hopefully be worth it.

Margie, the friend I made at LCC, and I decided since I'd need an able-bodied person to live with and she needed a place where her husband, Don, and kids could come for visits, that we would be roomies. Instead of paying her a wage, I'd pay all living expenses. With DVR paying my tuition, my disability social security check and a student loan we will manage. We still are going to have to be very frugal, but I am used to that.

During the summer we checked out several colleges. Some would not accept me; others had campuses either too large or too hilly. We settled on Central Washington College in Ellensburg, Wash., east of the Cascade Mountains. However, they would only admit me if I didn't expect or ask for any privileges that were not afforded to able-bodied students. Certainly a different outlook on disabilities than LCC.

Finding an accessible apartment for the three of us (Margie's little girl, Rhonda, will tag along while Dad and the other three stay in their nest in Kelso), we thought would be difficult and beyond our slender pockets of cash, but an acquaintance of Margie's has a son living there, and he has a small rental house. Thinking we were very lucky, we were appalled at the mess we encountered when we checked it out. Tiny can't even describe it and it was filthy. Their former renters were *definitely* not hygienic. Helen, the landlady, assured us that by the time we moved in, which will be right after Christmas, that she would have it in pristine shape plus her husband, Del, would build me a ramp. At this writing, we are hoping she kept her word.

The hated three quarters of chemistry are finished though I rather enjoyed organic chem. Aspirin, anyone? I learned to make it along with extracting caffeine from tea and coffee to compare which contains the most concentrate. Coffee won, tea has less per ounce. I can also make a nice wintergreen lotion. Passing students would comment, "You just came from Livermore's class, didn't you?" At least he didn't have us test dung.

Choosing a major has been exasperating. I'd love to teach, especially math, but that requires writing on blackboards, which is beyond my reach. They need to invent extension wheelchairs. I have finally decided on speech and hearing where I can work in a clinic with learning disabled children and people with head traumas.

Since I have only four years of DVR aid, I must go summers, also, plus I have to have a master's degree to work in a clinic. Five years in four is going to be a challenge, but I've found that in the last 14 years, I can handle most anything that gets in my way. Watch out Central kids, Shirley is on her way.

If you make it over the mountains, come by.

Let's hope for a prolific year for us all,

Shirley

CHRISTMAS 1970

Greetings From Ellensburg,

What a year this has been. Get a cup of coffee and sit down for this will be a long list of "happenings."

Two days after Christmas, we started over the pass in a heavy snowstorm, hauling our new washer/dryer and borrowed furniture in a pickup and the rest of our belongings in Margie's and Keith's cars. It was treacherous driving, but we made it without incident. True to her word, Helen (the landlady) had cleaned and spruced up the house. New linoleum, fresh paint on walls and cupboards greeted us. Her husband, Dell, had made a nice ramp so I got my first view of the house. Yup, it is still small. I can only turn around in the kitchen. Otherwise, I must back up to get out of the other rooms. After an overnight stay, the relatives went home leaving Margie, Rhonda and me on our own. Not much to do after putting away our few belongings, no TV hookup; therefore, we entertained ourselves playing games and attempting to construct a picture from a zillion little pieces of cardboard, namely a jigsaw puzzle.

Eventually, the big day was on the horizon. Margie put me to bed, set the alarm for six (first class at eight) and she herself retired. It seemed that I had hardly met up with the sandman when Margie was waking me. I was up, dressed and eating when I happened to glance at my watch. What, 4:00? Margie check your clock again. Sure enough it said 4:00, but she tuned into the radio station to make sure. Why did the alarm set for 6:00 go off at 4:00? Well, we never solved the clock problem, but here we were ready three hours before time to wake Rhonda and to leave.

Too much trouble for me to go back to bed so I drug out my latest novel (I must say here that it was the last novel reading I did for the next five months) while Margie went back to slumber land. Then it was actually time to go. Next dilemma, frozen car locks. Out came the hair dryer, locks got thawed, but by the time she got me settled in the car, they were frozen again, this time frozen inside of the door latch. Dryer didn't work this time. Margie then got a rope, tied it to her inside door handle, across both of us, and knotted it onto my door handle. At last we were off. A quick two miles to our first class, which luckily we had together. She intended to drop me off at the door and then park in the parking lot. OH YEAH! Gates were locked to all building areas within the campus. Pushing me through five inches of snow and sliding on icy sidewalks was a tough assignment for Margie. We finally reached our building only to find the door locked. Fifteen minutes in sub-freezing weather did not do wonders for our usual sunny dispositions. The prof showed up, did not apologize for being late, and we thawed out just in time to hit the sidewalks again. This time we had to go in separate directions. I begged a girl standing next to me to push me to my class. She was a sweetheart and promised to help each morning. Next class was up three flights of stairs. After pleading to several guys to be lifters and being rejected, I had made up my mind I was going to miss that class and get reassigned the next day to another when two fellows offered to help me up. This they did each morning the rest of the quarter. No moving classes downstairs to accommodate me at this lofty institution. They call it higher education, but I feel that is a misnomer for this college. They won't give an inch, not even when Margie begged the plant supervisor for a key to the gates.

Arriving home, we both were so dejected we could hardly talk civilly to each other. The next day went better, but that night we both confessed that had either of us said the day before, "Let's go home," we would have packed up and fled.

During the course of this year, I have been dumped in the snow, had Margie's car towed because we could not see the sign under a snow drift that said "No Parking," and nearly froze to death while waiting for Margie to pick me up. She bummed a ride to the tow company, which, after hearing the story, did not charge for the tow, although we were not so lucky at the police station. We still had to pay for the ticket, not easy on our meager budget.

Spring came. Snow melted, exhibiting toys, garbage, pots and numerous other items scattered throughout the yard. It took Margie and Rhonda all day to pick it up, sack it and take the trash to the dump.

Margie went home during Spring Break while I went to Benton City, Wash. to visit the Brenemans. A woman I had met from Richland offered to drive me, so I was happy not to have to go on the long ride over the icy pass again. We were following behind a car which had a small row boat tied on top, when all of a sudden, as we were crossing the Vantage Bridge, the dern boat decided after seeing water, that it belonged down there, dislodged itself, missed going to the water but instead landed in my windshield. Subsequently, my driver drove the rest of the way windshieldless with wind and bugs splaying across our faces.

At the Brenemans, I slept in Diane's bed while she bunked in with older sister, Linda. I was lying on my stomach reading when I detected a pitter pat across the bookshelf headboard. I looked up and there was a cute little field mouse that had ventured into the house sometime during the day. Thinking it would get into something it shouldn't, I yelled at Dick. He came in sleepily in his briefs, assessed the problem, grabbed the broom and started after the culprit. Delores and Linda both hearing the noise came to investigate and when learning of the situation, Delores locked herself into her bedroom and Linda landed on the kitchen table. Next came Billy, also in his unmentionables, with a logging boot. The poor frightened mouse ran every which way trying to escape these giant monsters. Finally he was subdued, killed and thrown out. An earthquake appeared to have hit that room as it was in such disarray. I am of the opinion that Dick was ready to smother me with one of the pillows when I asked, "Did you have to kill it?"

The Breneman's house sits on the bank of the Yakima River. which had frozen over about a foot thick for the first time in many years. On one of the mornings that I was there, it began to thaw and break up. Delores and I sat on the deck and watched as huge ice floes came roaring down river, mowing down trees along the banks as it surged by. What an eerie, but awesome, sound. There is no way to describe it.

Summer quarter is always short. We managed to have a few relaxing days—a picnic in the hills where we found some giant pine cones, Don and the kids came over for the Fourth of July where it snowed for two hours which it had never done before in recorded history, classes held in the shade of trees because of no A/C in buildings, and eating lots of cherries picked right from the orchards. Not a smart thing to do when one has not eaten such all winter. We blamed the smell on the cattle feedlot down the road. The kids stayed most of the summer, which was good for Margie and them. They missed their mom and she did likewise. The landlords have girls their ages so they had fun most nights sleeping out.

Our landlord's parents run a truck scale so they get a lot of produce given them when the loads are too heavy to pass state highway regulations. They in turn hand over to us an abundance of fresh corn, peas, and assorted fruits from the valley. It certainly helps the grocery bill.

I had a visiting prof from MIT teaching my psycholinguistics class. He was young, good looking and single, much to the delight of the three other girls in this hard, but fun, class. One lecture was on the difference in our English language in sections of the U.S. and also in different professions. One assignment was to write down some words used in a line of work or an area and see if the other students could determine what occupation or region it came from. I chose logging. Can you imagine the laughs I got when I had the prof write these words on the board?

whistle punk

choker

widow maker

sheep's cunt

donkey

No one, not even the prof, figured that one out. At the end of the quarter, this prof treated all nine of us (not many sign up for this difficult field of study) to a BBQ and drinks at his apartment. No, none of the girls got him.

Fall brought wind and it was dirty wind from farmers plowing their fields. The wind blows here so much that the trees all lean to one side, even this house does. If I don't set my brakes when sitting still, I roll into a corner.

Classes are better. I have only one upstairs and it has an elevator. I've made a lot of friends who are a great help to both Margie and I. I never lack for someone to push me from class to class.

This has practically turned into a book so will sign off by wishing you all the best holiday ever. I'm on the way to Keith and Marilyn's to do the same.

Love to all, Shirley, or Shitty, as three-year-old Steffanie calls me.

Me, Rose Bond & Helen Hoyer

The Graduates... Margie, Me, Sue

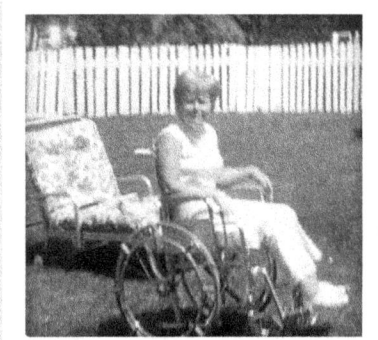

Hot Stuff!

Rhonda, Margie, Blair, Me

CHRISTMAS 1971

Dear Family and Friends,

Winter quarter was quite eventful as usual. Margie was pushing me to class one day when all of a sudden one of my front wheels went into a manhole that was hidden beneath a thin layer of snow, breaking the wheel off and dumping me head first into the frozen wasteland. A nice young man helped her get me into the chair and into a nearby building where they propped the chair, minus wheel, on top of some books while Margie went looking for a w/c shop to get the wheel repaired. They could not do such a job, but they did send her to an auto shop where they quickly restored the wheel to working order.

Since I'm very slow when writing, one of my better, empathetic profs, let me use a typewriter to take my essay tests in an adjacent room. On one such occasion, she got me set up, left the door open a smidgen in order for me to return the test when finished and went back to oversee her other charges. No sooner had she left than someone opened an outer door causing a gust of wind to pull mine shut. "No problem," I thought. "I'll just yell for someone in the hall to open it when I'm through." Time was up. Students burst from their classrooms. I yelled. No one heard me above all of the hubbub, and with my usual luck, the prof forgot me. There I sat with the last class of the day over in that building, in a tiny room with just a table, a typewriter, and a small window too high up to see out. Margie came to pick me up, and not finding me in my customary meeting place, started searching the campus to no avail. She called my prof... no answer. After several hours of both Margie and the campus guards looking, she tried the prof again. "Oh, my goodness," she screamed, "I don't remember her turning in her test." At last, after six hours of sitting in the dark, while wondering if I was going to spend the night with no company but flies, I was rescued.

I have one prof who stutters, but also has taken a dislike to me. Why? I haven't the slightest idea. Actually, it isn't just me, but also the other two older women in his class. And he is quite obvious about it. If he asks a question and we raise our hands, he ignores us. About once a month my legs get some muscle spasms causing them to tap, tap, tap on my footrest. This happened one day in his class. He turned to me and asked, "OK, Watson, what do you do for an encore?" Without thinking of the consequences, "I stutter," I replied. Of course everyone laughed and even clapped. However, it didn't help my grade, but I got a lot of satisfaction from it.

Margie and I usually go to the free (all several years old) movies on campus, but a movie came to the theater that we both wanted to see. Right in the middle of a love scene, my legs once again did their little dance, and we got the giggles. The couple in front of us mumbled something and proceeded to move further down the aisle. The legs relaxed and we continued to enjoy the movie.

Margie and I graduated with our BA's in June. Family and friends came from all over. I knew my sister, Gwenie, was coming from Denver but what a surprise it was when Jim also exited from the plane. As a brother in-law, no one could out do Jimbo, as I liked to call him. He spoiled me rotten whenever he was around. We had a big BBQ in our yard, visitors went home, and we began preparing for summer quarter.

I was beginning my MA, while Margie was getting a head start on hers. She already had a teaching job in Kelso, Wash. so we began looking for a replacement for her as my slave. Our landlady had an aunt who was interested in the job, and when the summer session was over, Mary and her seven-year-old boy moved in.

I really missed Margie and Rhonda when they departed. Her family had became my family.

Thanksgiving break came. A nice young man from Longview and a couple of gals from Centralia, Wash. drove me to Keith and Marilyn's to spend that holiday. On Sunday, we reversed the procedure only to find when I got back to my rental, Mary was gone and so was everything else. I had no food, no linens, no TV, and no pots, pans or cleaning supplies. She had taken everything but for the washer/dryer, bed, table, and couch. I'm sure she would have taken those if she had had a truck. Helen (the landlady) felt responsible as it was her aunt, but I assured her those things happen in the best of families. She rounded up some linen, helped me to bed, and spent the night. The next day, with Mary unable to be located, she called the police, but they said that with those items, unless my name was on them, it would be impossible to trace them to her. Helen and I went to a thrift shop and a grocery where she insisted on replacing everything.

I started looking for other help, and in the meantime, Delores's daughter, Linda, came and spent a week. We did fine but for one little incident. Chair in place, she heaved me out of the car, missed the chair and sat me on the pavement. A male student assessing the problem ran to assist her. I'm sure that the fact she is very pretty helped the matter. This also reminds me of the day Margie did the same thing. She had positioned the chair, set the brakes, went to transfer me, but there was no chair. The wind had blown it clear to the back of her car. You cannot beat Ellensburg's winds.

I was getting desperate for help when Jan, one of my classmates, offered to take me on, as she was interested in going into nursing.

Now it is time to go back to Longview for Christmas break. Hopefully, my next year will be less stressful. One can only look back and laugh. I can imagine that is what all of you are doing.
TA TA

Love from the worn-out student, Shirley

The Daily News — Longview, Washington — Thursday, November 9, 1972 — 14

LCC graduate Shirley Watson gets master's degree, seeks job

Text and photographs
By VERA MORGAN

It's quite something to be named "Handicapped Woman of the Year" by the Governor's Committee on Employment of the Handicapped — to be honored at a luncheon — cited for outstanding accomplishment — presented with a bronze plaque marking the event — to be the target of both still and TV cameras and the vortex of a banquet room full of smiling spectators.

The object of all that glamorous glorification is Shirley Watson, of Longview, a young woman who enrolled in Lower Columbia College in December 1967.

She had been out of circulation for the previous 11 years as the result of a disabling automobile accident. The discipline of study had long been forgotten, but the challenge of competing with students many years her junior didn't bother her. She had her sights trained on the distant future, and a degree in speech therapy.

After graduation from LCC, Shirley, with Mrs. Don (Margie) Young of Kelso as attendant-companion-chauffeur, set off for Ellensburg, where both young women entered Central Washington State College. These two weren't run-of-the-orchard young students on their first venture away from home.

They were mature young women: Margie the mother of four school-age children (one of whom, 10-year-old Rhonda, accompanied them on the Ellensburg expedition); Shirley the wheelchair-bound young matron whose schooling was to be complicated by harder work, and a few hazards she thus far had not envisioned.

Ellensburg's wintry weather alone was a factor none too well understood by either of these Western Washingtonians. They soon learned, however, that folding wheelchairs can freeze fast overnight in a car, and that icy ruts can snap off chair wheels and lip the passenger into a snowbank. They also learned that a flight of 60-odd stairs to a classroom can baffle otherwise helpful, gallant, strong young men.

But it took more than architectural barriers and difficult subjects like physiology, pathology, and psychology to deter Shirley. So she went to Tacoma to fulfill the student teaching requirement of her college course by 1971 and in the Franklin Pierce School District she helped youngsters at the Central Avenue School to overcome minor speech defects.

Thus she earned her bachelor's degree and a provisional teaching certificate.

Still not satisfied, Shirley liked the prospect of an M.S. degree, and in June decided to bypass vacation in favor of summer school, to shorten the interval between herself and that M.S.

The gap has closed. Shirley received her master's degree in her science specialty, speech therapy, in the spring of 1972.

When the 1972 vacation-time rolled around, did Shirley just sit there?

Yes, she sat there. At her typewriter, writing 163 letters of application to institutions all over the United States. Then she sat there reading 149 replies, some of which made those aforementioned architectural barriers seem even more insurmountable, when the writers said, "Our building not accessible to wheelchairs." Among the 149 letters were only two "possibles." There was a single firm offer, but even that was contingent upon a grant now long overdue.

We now come to the memorable Olympia luncheon.

Mrs. Sheileaes Dunn, chairman of the Women's Division of the governor's committee, gave a brief resume of Shirley's life since her disabling injury, while Gov. Evans looked on — himself in a wheelchair for the day with assimulated "disability." In presenting the plaque, Mrs. Dunn said, "Despite all of her difficulties, this courageous, determined young woman never faltered. She surmounted obstacles that would discourage even the able bodied."

Afterwards, Shirley was heard to say, "I felt like the leading lady in 'This Is Your Life' TV show. It was a lovely tribute." Then she added, "But I hope some day to be recognized for my ability in my chosen field, rather than for my disability."

Shirley Watson certainly has done her part. She has justified the confidence shown in her by the Washington State Division of Vocational Rehabilitation, who sponsored her rehabilitative therapy at Good Samaritan Hospital in Puyallup, then her schooling both LCC and CWSC.

Any community could do with more Shirley Watsons.

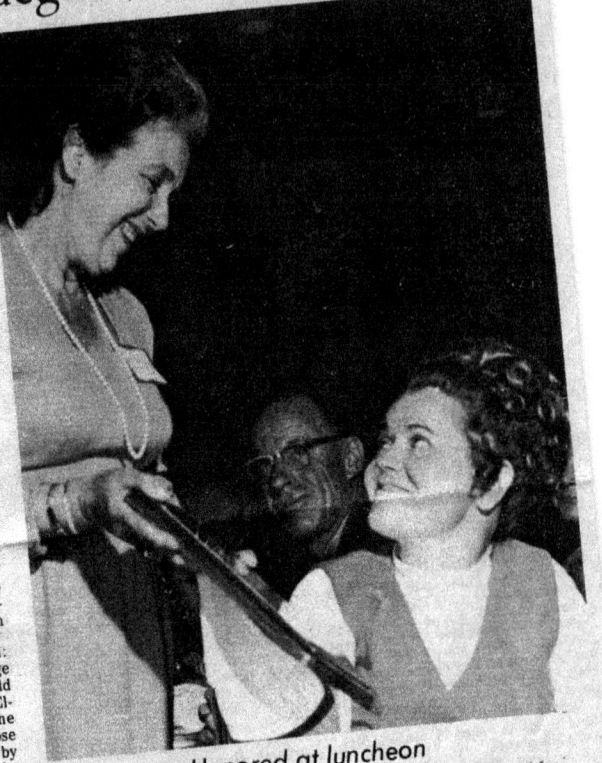

Honored at luncheon

Shirley Watson (seated), "Handicapped Woman of the Year" for the state of Washington, receives the commemorative plaque from Mrs. Sheileaes Dunn, chairman of the Women's Division, the Governor's Committee on Employment of the Handicapped. Mrs. Watson was honored at the committee's luncheon Oct. 4.

CHRISTMAS 1972

Hi Everyone,

Jan proved to be a fine companion, but I still missed Margie and her family. I had become a silent witness to them deciding whether Mark was allowed to wear his hair long to Sandy being allowed to date.

After writing last year's letter, I spent what was supposed to be a week in Tacoma General Hospital for a urinary procedure, but which became a month as I contracted Asian flu. They refused to let me go until my temp went back to normal. Because it got so high, my hair vanished. With a friend's help, I purchased a wig, and returned to school two weeks late, but my profs let me make up the work providing I got it in within a week.

Rose and her sister, Barb, came to spend a few days in Feb. Since I had been wearing the wig for over a month, it was becoming quite rank. I asked Barb, a beautician, if it could be washed. She graciously said she'd take care of it. However, upon arising the next morning, it was not dry. "I'll fix that", she said and promptly threw it into my dryer. You've seen pictures of cats touching an electric socket; that is what my tresses looked like after their stint in that machine. She brushed, she combed and even dampened them down, but those synthetic locks refused to be subdued. There was nothing to do but to go to class Aunt Jemima style until I once again sported hair.

The college library was my second home, for much research had to be done for my thesis. On one occasion, I had to go to the second floor. Intending to wait for another student to enter and push the 2nd floor button for me, I entered the elevator. It was only after the door went shut that I remembered that there was a sign by it stating that all able bodied students had to use the stairs. Once again, I was in a tiny enclosure waiting to be rescued. Fifty-five minutes later, a worker bent on restocking a cart of books upstairs entered and saved me from another campus search.

Spring quarter, I spent off campus gathering information for my thesis. I stayed with my former rehab PT and spent my days working with aphasics (people who have lost their speech due to brain injuries, usually strokes) trying to help them restore a semblance of communication with others. Many of these patients get very frustrated and depressed. One such guy was John who would let loose with curses, mainly the "F" word. After such a barrage of expletives, I told him when he needed to say that word to hold up his thumb instead of spewing out the unacceptable expression, which he did from then on. I doubt it worked at home, but it surely did in the clinic.

Thesis done and submitted only to find it had to be revised and revised. No way was I able to type it over several times, so I did what most do, hired a student who did this to keep himself in food. Orals were not fun, mainly because my former stuttering professor was on the thesis committee. He, I'm sure, was determined to keep me from passing. He asked questions that had nothing to do with my work. This is not allowed. Finally, another member chastised him. I survived and passed.

During the summer, I finished and received the big MA; I then started looking for a job. After sending out over two hundred letters, I got only two interviews. One was in a clinic in Snohomish, Washington; the other was for a military hospital. Neither one panned out. They just didn't think I was capable of doing the job from a w/c.

This was also the year that the bill was passed in Congress that all public buildings had to be w/c accessible. Guess who came running to me to see what was needed to meet the requirements? Yup, the campus supervisor. Instead of laughing in his face as I felt like doing, I "diplomatically" told him of barriers that would have made my two years there much easier: ramps on sidewalks and into buildings, classes downstairs, the bookstore with a door without a turnstile, and most important, keys to the gates. Time will tell if they get done.

Rose had asked the superintendent at the school where she worked as a secretary if I could sub until a job came up for a speech and hearing teacher.

So here I am at Rose's hoping a real job opens by next year.

A little laughable matter before closing. Rose's neighbor's house caught fire. She forgot she had started running bath water for one of the kids, and they all ran over to watch the firemen doing their job. Water kept running in the tub and every minute I expected to see it start spilling out into the hallway. Upon returning to the house, she got it turned off before disaster struck, but she said it probably would not have held another cupful.

Eating dinner one night, I choked on some meat cutting off my breath. After several tries to get Rose's attention and deciding I was soon to meet my maker or the devil, she saw what was happening and began pounding on my back while yelling, "I don't know what to do," several times before sending one of her kids go get an EMT neighbor. He yanked me out of the chair, deposited me on the floor and pushed on my diaphragm. Problem solved. Once again I fooled the powers that be by staying alive. After thanking Mr. Carpenter, I asked Rose why she was shouting. Her answer, "I guess I thought if you couldn't talk, you couldn't hear either."

Have a super Christmas.

Love to all, Shirley

My closet sized classroom

Finally teaching!

Drawing by a student of mine...

My little house

CHRISTMAS 1973

Greetings from Toledo High School.

Yup, I am now a full-fledged special education teacher in the high school resource room.

In the spring, after having a teaching job promised (more on that later), I felt I had enough money left from my inheritance from my dad that I could find a place of my own and hire help. I found a cute little house in the country with NO STAIRS; then I put an ad in our neighboring papers and also one in Seattle to hire a "girl Friday." I got calls from street people, those whom I could tell were inebriated and even one from a gay guy. I guess I wouldn't have to worry about him seducing me, but didn't think the school would look kindly on a man sharing my abode. After interviewing a couple, Rose talked to a lady who had moved to Longview from Kansas, liked her, and I hired her. So Jessie, a motherly and sweet lady, is my now right and left hand.

Now to the job. The Chehalis School Dist. who hire and supervise all of the county special education staff accepted me. Since neither Toledo nor neighboring Winlock High School had SP. ED. (special education) programs, it was my job to establish a curriculum and teach a half-day in each. As do all sp. ed. teachers, I have an aide, Jan Vineyard, who works with me at both schools, and besides being my hands, legs and sometimes brains, she also is my chauffeur. She picks me up each morning, drives me to both schools and assists the students and me. Winlock HS presented no problem as it had a nice large room with no stairs in their one-story new building, but Toledo tendered another, but not insurmountable, situation. My assigned room was down a flight of stairs and was formerly the sick room with dimensions of about 6' by 10'. The principal assigned two football players to lug me down, plus I had to be in and situated behind my tiny table in the 'classroom' before students entered. There was no room for a desk for either the students or me. They, in turn, had to do their work on little lap tables the shop teacher quickly nailed together for the eight students I had during each class period, 24 in all. Thankfully, I had no students that first two weeks as materials had to be gathered, students tested, and schedules arranged. The only advantages of being in Toledo HS is that this is the school I attended for my junior high and high school enlightenment, graduating in 1953, making me feel more comfortable here, plus our little room has its own restroom.

Each day goes like this:

1. Get up and ready.

2. Jan picks me up after Jessie drives me to the THS parking lot; they exchange vehicles and Jan drives me to WHS.

3. Teach English, reading and math with materials I have to make up as WHS, being new, has no money left for a newly mandated SP. ED. Program.

4. Drive to THS.

5. Steve Seacrest and Kenny Shipp hoist me downstairs. Jan and I have 10 min. to gobble our sandwiches.

6. Teach English, math, reading. Good materials. (Later I sneaked some out to use at WHS.)

7. Kenny and Steve reverse the stair lift up.

8. Reverse driving situation.

8. Home to do paper work. Sp. Ed. teachers have extra paper work, as we must document each day what we have accomplished with each student.

At the beginning of December, I was given my choice of the two schools I wanted to stay with throughout the day, as the state had come through with funds for a full time teacher in each school. Even though the facilities are not as convenient as WHS's, I chose THS as I feel comfortable here and the staff are more accommodating.

At each school, I had started the year out by telling the students why I was in a w/c, and then asked if they had any questions. Most were general questions as to how I managed dressing, driving, etc. but I had to stifle a laugh when one student asked if I didn't get tired of sitting all of the time... like I have a choice.

My little, or should I say BIG, darlings range from those who are just behind in reading and math to a few who have emotional problems. Some love the special attention; others are embarrassed. The latter being the school's more popular souls. I have found that fifty percent of my job consists of counseling. I had one boy in WHS who was so emotionally disturbed that he would just sit in the back of the room doing nothing but staring out of the window. Several times, I kept him after class and tried to get him to talk to me to no avail. Two weeks ago, he hung himself. I'm not sure I can handle this job if I continue to have others like him.

It is wonderful to have a reason to rise each morning, to live on my own and have a check at the end of the month. I still have to be frugal. My paycheck is $685. Rent is $150 (this includes utilities), Jessie's wages are $250, and that leaves the rest for food and gas. But I love, love, love being independent; part of that is now I have a motorized chair that DVR bought for me so I could move more than a few paces by myself. Son picked it up in Longview and the whole family delivered it to me. Each kid wanted to try it out, even before I had my turn, they had instructions that if they ran into anything, out they would go. After each kid tried out the chair, it was my turn. Guess who was the first to hit something? Yes, 'twas me. All of them in unison said, "Aunt Shirley, out you go."

My brother Keith came to visit. We were chatting in the living room when Jesse, in a shaky voice, said, " Shirley, you have a snake on the back of your chair." Since Jesse sometimes likes to kid me, I replied, "OK, tell me another one." She was adamant that she was telling the truth and enlisted Keith to look. He assured me there really was as he picked it up and showed me. That little reptile had apparently slithered up onto my battery case while I was outside earlier. I HATE SNAKES, and that is because as a kid, when we lived in Southern Idaho, my brother, Addy, and my older-than-me niece, Dell, used to tease me by throwing the bull snakes at me.

We've had some excitement in the neighborhood even though we are supposed to be living in the quiet country. My landlady's house caught fire burning the upper floor, but they were able to save the rest.

During one night in the summer, I heard a vehicle that sounded mighty close to my bedroom window. I had Jesse get up and look. She saw a strange truck in the field, and not knowing what else to do as the landlady was gone, I called the sheriff who happened to have a deputy fairly close. That truck happened to have a prime beef already loaded. Cattle rustlers in this day? It was a page right out of an old western novel.

With that I say Merry Christmas and love to all.

Mrs. Watson, teacher

CHRISTMAS 1974

Dear Family and Friends,

After 1-1/2 years, I think I have this teaching venture a "little" bit organized. Without a curriculum to go by as most teachers have, I continue to have to search out resources on my own. This is an individualized program; therefore, I have students on every level in the basics. Some can only read on second or third grade level, but do well in math; with others it is the opposite. My evenings are taken up with searching out materials with which they can succeed. Plus, in order to get government funding for this program, there is the multitude of paper work. My days are long, but it surely beats the alternative.

Kenny and Steve continue to ferry me down and up stairs. They will graduate this year, but not to worry. Next fall, our new school will open with NO stairs and a bathroom I can get into. A big plus is that I will be able to use my motorized chair. It will be nice to go to the students, not them to me.

My room being in the basement, the window opens onto the lawn. As it was a hot day, we had the window open, and while I was helping Ricky, Art climbed out the window and vamoosed. Jan climbed out after him, brave of her as he was twice her size, but could not catch him. He never did come back to school. He was a troubled boy who has a record of petty crimes. I tried but could not make a difference with him. This is the same kid who swilled down too much wine during lunch, entered my room, and before sitting down, upchucked wine mixed with hot dogs. YUK!

Pierce County Herald — Oct. 30, 1974

Nothing Stops Shirley Watson

Wheelchair Whirlwind Earns Her Way!

Story and photographs by
Vera Morgan

If there were such a degree as "W.W", Shirley Watson could rightfully add it to the three earned M.S. after her name W.W. for Wheelchair Whirlwind!

When Shirley Watson was wheeled into Good Samaritan Hospital's Rehabilitation Center in 1967, she knew what to expect. In the eleven years since an automobile accident had left her quadriplegic, she had undergone rehabilitative therapy in other hospitals: In Oregon (Good Samaritan Hospital at Portland); Washington (the former McCord Air Force Base Hspital); and Texas (Brooks Hospital in San Antonio). Yet she could tolerate her wheelchair less than two hours a day.

"Well, here we go again," she thought, upon entering Puyallup's "Good Sam." And a rigorous, exhausting "go" it was, for three months. Intensive therapy on an eight - hours - a - day schedule, five days a week. No reprieve except to attend a brother's funeral in Idaho.

I remember when I first met Shirley, in 1967. She'd just had a strenuous session on the gym mat. She sagged. Her hair was disheveled. Her clothing was twisted and wrinkled. But her good disposition was intact -- or else she was too tired to resist when I interviewed her and asked to take pictures.

By the time Shirley's treatment had "toughened" her enough to endure her wheelchair for ten to twelve hours without exhaustion, she was ready to move back into circulation.

Returned to Puyallup

I pursued Shirley with note book and camera from that time to this, while she pursued her higher education and dreamed of independence. Lower Columbia College at Longview. Then Central Washington State. To fulfill the student teaching requirement for her teacher's certificate, Shirley returned to Puyallup, and helped children in the Franklin Pierce School District with minor speech defects. Finally she went back to Ellensburg where, after having studied even during vacations, she earned her M.S. degree in speech therapy.

During her year of graduate study, Shirley spent her spare time writing 163 letters of application to institutions throughout the United States, seeking a job anywhere available. It must have taxed her courage to read the 149 replies: all negative except two. Excuses ranged from Shirley's lack of experience to the lack of elevators in buildings thereby rendered "inaccessible to wheelchairs." Eventually the two "maybe" letters failed to produce a job.

It was enough to defeat even an ablebodied person.

A glimmer of hope came when Governor Daniel J. Evans' Committee on Employment of the Handicapped named Shirley Watson "Handicapped Woman of the Year." (1972) But the glimmer died with the expiring flashes of news cameras at the Awards Luncheon in Olympia. The doubtful honor produced neither employment nor job interview in the months to come.

The indomitable Shirley finally got a job (although not in her specialty) on her own initiative, and has just begun her second year as the source teacher of educationally handicapped young people at Toledo (Washington) High School. Ironically, THAT school has an architectural barrier: a flight of stairs leading to the resource classroom in the basement! But the school also has strong and willing students to carry Shirley and her wheelchair down and up.

Shirley Watson might be looked upon as Washington's counterpart of Jill Kinmont, the former Olympic Games ski contestant. Both young women became quadriplegic as the result of accidents: Jill's the more glamorous mishap, while skiing; Shirley's the result

AFTER unceasing effort on her part, Shirley finally succeeded in getting a job as resource teacher of educationally handicapped young people at Toledo High School.

of an automobile accident. But there the analogy ends.

Nationwide publicity brough Jill offers of employment. A recent TV interview revealed Jill's salary as $19,000 a year; and the same TV program showed her mother transferring Jill from wheelchair to bed, the inference being that the mother is Jill's attendant and housekeeper.

The salary for Shirley Watson's self-acquired job falls short of Jill Kinmont's by several thousand dollars. And Shirley's salary must cover the services of a full-time attendant-housekeeper, as well as rent and other normal living expenses, plus taxi fare or driving fees when the volunteer services of friends competent to handle Shirley and her folding wheelchair are not readily available.

I consider Shirley Watson the most courageous person I've ever known. Confronted with such obstacles and frustrations as she has faced, I'd long since have thrown in the sponge.

Shirley's Dream

Know what Shirley's current dream is? To me, it sounds impossible of attainment. But to Shirley, it's just another goal. She wants a wheelchair van, no less, so she can dispense with hired taxi service and no longer be frequently dependent upon friends to take her between home, school, and necessary meeting and appointments.

A wheelchair van, custom made to Shirley's physical requirements, can cost upwards of $7,500. But chances are someday you will see that van tooling along with Shirley and her indispensable wheelchair in the driver - seat space...

Shirley's Therapy at Good Samaritan Hospital, and her subsequent college education, were sponsored by the Washington State Division of Vocational Rehabilitation.

Article in the Pierce County Herald. I'm famous!

NAMED Handicapped Woman of the Year for Washington State in 1972, Shirley attended the Awards Luncheon in Olympia accompanied by Mrs. Rose Bond, a long-time friend from Toledo. With them is James Campbell, chairman of Governor Daniel J. Evans' Committee on Employment of the Handicapped.

Rose and I attending a luncheon in Olympia where I was honored as Handicapped Woman of the Year in 1972 (part of article, opposite page).

We had to take the kids to the library while the janitor cleaned the up the mess and made an effort to fumigate the room However, that smell lingered for some time. One can only laugh.

One of my students came to me a couple of days ago and said, "Mrs. Watson, you had better talk to Jim Bob." Jim Bob has this nickname because of his resemblance to Jim Bob of the Waltons. I asked him what the problem was; he said he couldn't tell me. "But how can I talk to him if I don't know what is going on," I replied. He relented. Apparently some boys, when the teacher was called to the office, and knowing Jim Bob would do anything to be 'one of the boys', told him to yell across the room to a girl and say, "Hey, Lisa, wanna f..k." Of course everyone laughed and Jim Bob thought he was a hit. On my prep period, I had Jan write the word in big letters on the board with the intention of calling Jim Bob to my room to explain that that was not proper language to use anywhere, especially at school. But before he got to my room, the teacher next door, who was very religious as well as stern, walked into my room, took one glance at the board and remarked, "I always wondered what you taught in here." Before I could explain, he left. He will probably mention that often over the years until he retires.

Jesse decided, after a year, she couldn't stand living amidst our forests, crooked roads and big hills and moved back home. After all, she came from Kansas with few trees and roads that go north, south, east and west in straight lines and just a few small hills. Here we would call their hills, bumps. She said all the green made her nauseous and all the trees made her claustrophobic.

Enter LaDonna. She had been my student aide last year and knew I needed a new attendant. She is married with a little three-year-old boy and a husband in the service in Germany. Since Nicholas, alias Boomer, has been here, he has written on one of my paintings with crayon, dumped charcoal on the living room carpet, and climbed into a tree (we still cannot figure out how he got there) mainly to get the neighbor's cat that he probably chased up there in the first place. You can see why he got the nickname. However, he can be such a cutie and loves to climb into my lap to give hugs.

So goes my life for this past year.

Have a wonderful NEW YEAR.

Love to all,

Shirley, the frustrated teacher

CHRISTMAS 1975

Greetings from the new workplace.

We've moved into our new high school—no stairs, wide halls, many, big windows and best of all, I have a large room with lots of storage space, desks for all, including me, AND an office. I now can use my motorized chair at school, but must leave it there as is doesn't exactly fit into my Chevy sedan. However, at home, I can move myself in my push chair for a short distance.

One morning I came to work to find my chair battery dead. I usually plug it into my charger a couple of times a week before leaving for home. Since I had done that just two days before, it should not have been without its morning juice. During the day, the mystery was solved when one of my athletic students said, "Mr. K and Mr. Hippi sure had fun doing time trials in your chair." Apparently these young coaches didn't realize I would have to be hooked up to my charger while making an effort to teach. You never saw such sheepish grins when I asked them who won.

LaDonna's husband has returned home. Enter Julie, whom we secretly called Jerky, so-named as she makes some strange choices. We had been to Chehalis to get groceries. I had bought a box of oranges to share with Rose. After delivering her half, we returned home. Julie was putting the groceries away while I was correcting papers at the kitchen table. I was getting concerned as to what was going on when Julie kept sighing. Finally I asked her what her problem was. "I can't get this box in the fridge," she groaned. After explaining to her that she needed to take them out of the box and to put them in the fruit and veggie drawer, I went back to my papers. Again with the sighs. "Now what is the matter?" I asked. "I can't get them all in here. What should I do with these six?" Exasperated that she couldn't figure out to just put them on a shelf, I replied, "Eat them." "All six?" she asked.

Another day we were shopping in Longview with me giving her driving directions. "Turn left," I said meaning at the next light. However, she immediately turned left driving onto a cement divider, high centering us and necessitating having to call a wrecker to get us off the divider and both on our appointed rounds. I'm usually a very patient person, but I couldn't handle having her with me after several other ridiculous situations: running us off the road and into a tree to avoid a bird, waxing herself into a corner when doing the kitchen floor not knowing how to get out of the situation and locking herself out of the house not only once but three times. I had to look for a more reliable attendant.

Enter Evelyn. I had put an ad in the Portland paper. She and a young couple had traveled from back east to Portland where the young couple was getting a new job. Evelyn was looking for some kind of employment while waiting to get her hair styling license in Wash., saw my ad and called. Because she was my age, I felt we'd make a good match, and we did. Before coming west, she had become disillusioned with a religious cult she had been in and left; however, she still walked up and down the road counting her beads and chanting. Nevertheless, we got along great. After all, it had been my dream to have my own hairdresser and make-up girl. I knew it would be a short stay and she left after four months when she found a job in Calif. working in a high-class shop. I really miss her.

Before Evelyn left, she helped me move into a duplex in town where it would be more accessible to the school. The sister of an old high school friend of mine owns it.

Now I have Susan, who wants to go to nursing school. If she can care for me, she said, she would know for sure. She is smart, sweet and fun. Because she goes home on weekends, I also have

Rose's daughter, Shirley, filling in. She is very young, just 11, but she does a superb job.

Time for bed.

Merry Christmas to all.

Love,

Shirley

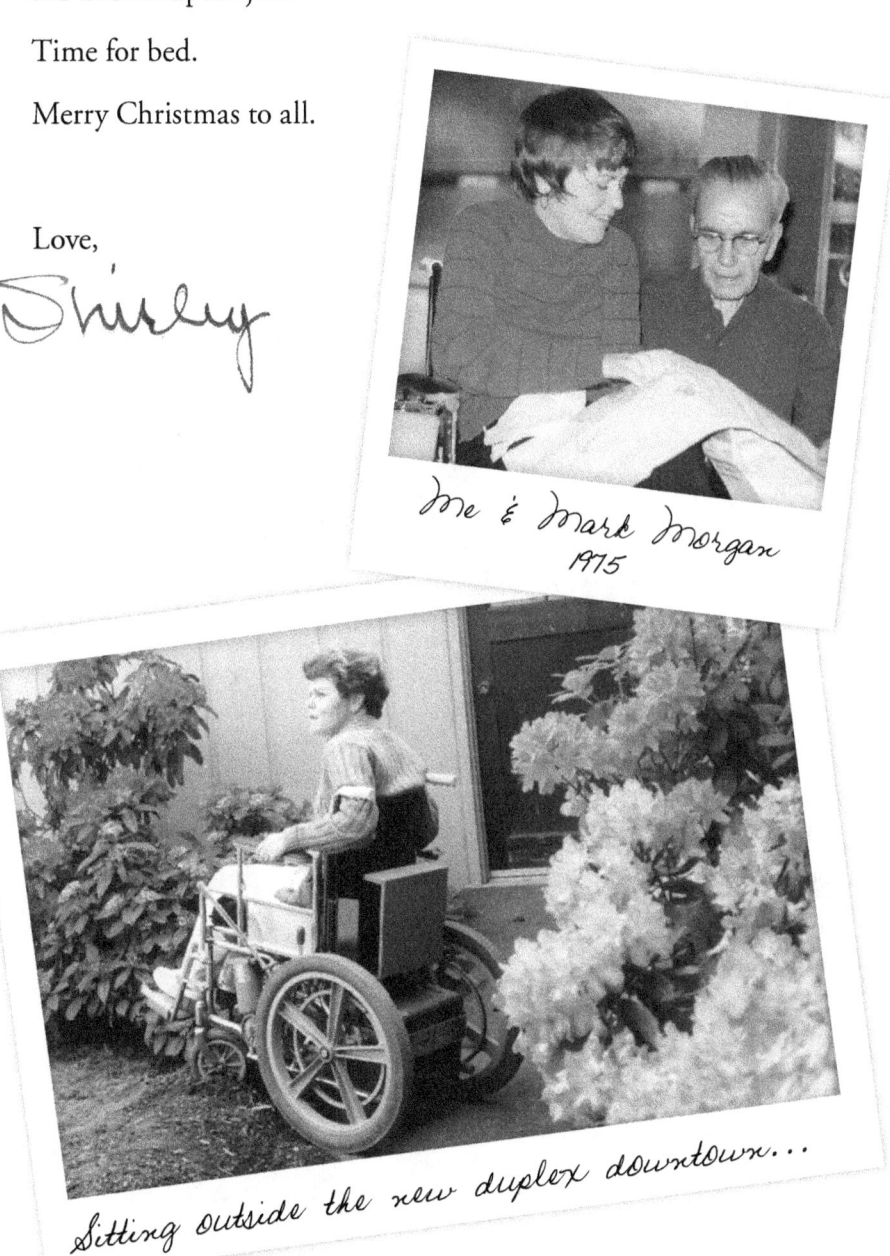

Me & Mark Morgan 1975

Sitting outside the new duplex downtown...

What kind of dragging noise?

CHRISTMAS 1976

Season's Greetings to One and All,

Once again I have new help. Susan left to move to Olympia and nursing school at St. Martin's College. Margie's daughter, Sandy, finished high school in the spring, moved in, and started college at Lower Columbia where Margie and I did our first two years. She is tiny but mighty.

Our first experience happened in the middle of the night. I sleep on my stomach and sometimes I need to turn onto my side. I can do this by getting up on my elbows, and with a huge push, I can move my dead weight over. But that night, I misjudged the distance and rolled off the bed landing between it and the wall. After yelling for Sandy several times, she finally came running. She said her heart quit and her stomach fell to the floor when she looked and I wasn't there. "Where are you?" she yelled. A miracle?? Had I gotten up and walked? No such luck. After locating me, she picked me up and threw me back in bed. Adrenaline must have kicked in as she is probably on the minus side of 100 lb.

My friendly DVR man paid me a visit asking if I'd like a van that they would purchase for me, which I could wheel right in and out of. Did he think I'd actually say no? I could hardly wait for the day for it to be delivered. No more transferring from chair to car and vice versa. Eventually my cream-colored Royce Mobile arrived. It is quite unique. The side door, instead of sliding, folds down to the ground making a ramp. A button inside, and also one on the outside, do this automatically. I now go places

I ordinarily wouldn't have, as it was such a pain to transfer. My only problem is that I have to sit behind the front seats, making it impossible to see much as I sit so high. We christened her "Mona."

Because money is tight for both of us, we have to pinch our pennies to be able to once a month go to a movie or have a hamburger. To do this, we play one game of cribbage a night... loser pays a penny for each point she loses by and a quarter if she is skunked. Winnings go into a jar. Usually it is just a few cents, but every so often, one of us has to shell out that big coin. Needless to say, we surely delight in our reward.

On one of Shirley's weekends, we were sitting at the kitchen table when smoke started rolling up from behind me. My chair was telling me something. "Get me out of here!" I yelled. Promptly, Shirley opened the door and shoved me outside. "I meant out of the chair." I said. Luckily it was just the wiring, and it had already quit smoking. A trip to the w/c shop, and we were good to go again.

For Thanksgiving, I was invited to Sandy's parents. For our contribution to the dinner, Sandy made a pecan pie. I'd never made one and neither had she. We kept looking at it, as it seemed to be taking as long for the middle to cook as it took Methuselah to die. Ultimately the center solidified. At the Young's, dessert time came. We heard Don and Margie conversing in the kitchen then laughing. Shortly, Don arrived with the pie and a SAW. Not a prudent way of letting us know that that darn pie sets up in the middle 'after' it cools. Needless to say, no one ventured to break his or her teeth on it. However, it did look pretty.

A knock at the door. I opened it to find the policeman who lives across the street. My heart stopped. Who had died? What had happened to someone I love? However, he asked what I planned to do with the plants in my front planter. Strange request. "Nothing, but why do you ask?" said I. "Do you need them for pain relief?" he asked. "What? They just came up, I thought they were pretty," I replied. After some discussion, I found they were marijuana plants, but how they got there, I did not know. He took care of them, but told me I might ask if anyone had seen kids around my house in the spring.

Jan, my aide at school, had left at the end of the school year of '74. I now have Kay, the daughter-in-law of an old friend. She is smart with a dry sense of humor, which my students love. Because I'm supposed to drink a lot of water, I keep a hot pot in my room where it is handy. One day a student asked if I'd like him to pour me a cup to which I agreed. Just as I went to take a sip, I noticed that it had a tinge of yellow to it. I quietly said to Kay that I didn't think I had better drink it and she agreed. I got even more suspicious when Rick or one of his two buddies, kept asking me if I was going to drink the water Rick had so graciously offered me. I assured them that I would get to it. Bell rang, class changed. I asked Kay to look in the pot. Those darn kids had sneakily dropped marijuana leaves into it. Then it dawned on me where my house plants had come from. After school, I inquired of my principal as to what I should do about this incident. "Since you didn't drink any, you ruined their fun. Just don't say anything." Case closed.

We are looking forward to Christmas break. I'll spend it this year with the Bonds.

Blessings to all,

Shirley, the almost druggie teacher

My first road trip "for fun," post accident...

CHRISTMAS 1977

In June, the first students I had as freshmen graduated. Only seven of the eleven made it through, but that is to be expected when the majority come from dysfunctional families or are so far behind that they give up.

After saving my tax returns for the last four years and scrimping on other entertainment, Sandy, Shirley and I left Toledo behind for my first long journey for fun, post accident. Because they are young and neither had been far away from home, it promised to be quite an adventure.

Our first overnight stop was in Boise at Dale and Phyllis's. The second night, Sandy decided to go partying with my niece, Lynda. I was not in the mood and Shirley was too young to go into the nightclub where they were planning to whoop it up. And whoop it up they did; however, Sandy didn't much like the idea of us getting up at six the next morning since she didn't get in until three, but she HAD BEEN WARNED.

We left Boise and turned north at Mt. Home heading for Sun Valley. Upon our arrival there, Sandy claimed she was too tired to sightsee but relented when Shirley told her she would push her in my manual chair, which I'd brought along to be able to get into places with stairs; the motorized one being an exercise of futility for the able bodied. With both of us in chairs, people either stared or questioned why. With one inquisitive couple, and before I could explain, Sandy quipped, "She is my mother and we've been in an accident." The couple empathized, chatted for a bit, and we went our separate ways. The next morning (we spent the night in a ski lodge), we stopped at a grocery in Haley to buy lunch and dinner provisions for our cooler. Of course, Sandy had recuperated by that time and was walking. As we rounded an aisle, whom should we bump into but the empathetic couple from Sun Valley. With sheepish grins, we said, "Hi?" and hot-footed it out of there. No miracle, just one "party pooper."

Next stop was Craters of the Moon. It was extremely hot, so I stayed in the air-conditioned gift shop while the other two toured the lava beds and caves. The guide warned them it would be cold in the caves, but they never expected it to be below freezing. Both came out with giant goose bumps.

We stopped in Rigby to visit a childhood friend of mine, then on to Pocatello. We spent almost a week there as I have three brothers and their families and several cousins who live in the area, drove to McCammon, my childhood town, to show the girls my old home, school etc. and visited a few old friends. It is amazing how a town 'shrinks' in size after you move away at age 12 and revisit as an adult.

We left Poky and headed for Denver via Wyoming. Because I misjudged driving time, it was getting dark, and we had yet to get to Cheyenne where we had motel reservations. As Sandy drove along, we kept hearing a thump, thump. Thinking we had a flat tire, I had them get out and look. No flat tire, just a lot of dead jackrabbits and squirrels. There was no way to miss hitting them unless the driver swerved into the sagebrush where we'd have to spend the night with them AND the coyotes. Sandy refused to go on and finally coerced Shirley into driving to our destination.

We arrived at my sister Gwen's the next day only to discover Sandy's bathing suit missing which she insisted was not ripped off by some handsome wooer in the motel pool. Jim and Gwen were great hosts treating us to a night at Elitche's Gardens and Amusement Park where both girls had their first roller coaster ride and a lunch at Casa Bonita. The Casa Bonita is a fun restaurant where, while you watch, they make sopapillas—two squares of sweet dough pressed together around the sides and dropped into hot grease causing them to puff up with a hollow between layers. You bite off the corners and fill them with honey, yummy. We watched cliff divers and listened to strolling musicians. On our own, we went up Lookout Mountain to check out Buffalo Bill's grave and museum and also to Red Rocks Amphitheater, a theater where seats and stage are all carved from a hill of red stone.

(I am so thankful we decided to go to Denver, as in the initial planning, we weren't sure we'd have enough gas and motel money to last us. Two weeks after we were there, my sweet brother-in-law, Jim, went to the hospital for a simple hernia operation, got up to go to the bathroom, had a blood clot hit his brain and died instantly.)

The next two days were spent traveling to Reno. We didn't think much of that town so went on to Lake Tahoe. We got tickets that afternoon for an evening show; Sandy and I gambled our $20 each (Shirley being too young), and ate our lunch outside. Just before we were to go in for the show, I noticed something on the skirts of both girls' white dresses. GUM! They were incensed to think someone would put their gum where others would obviously sit. However, with ice and good old adhesive remover, both were placated. As we entered the theater, what should we find but stairs. The usher insisted that he was not going to try and get others to help lift me and chair up that short flight of stairs. Since we had scrimped in order to buy tickets, we were not going to let this insensitive man stop us. We asked for the manager. He obliged us by wheeling me through the cloakroom, garbage room, kitchen and finally the seating area. Our tickets were for seating close to the stage. We were told, however, that I could not sit in an aisle, but would have to sit in the back of the theater. So much for abiding by the ADA law. I've learned a lesson. Check out w/c seating before buying.

Back in Reno, we bought eight cases of Coors, requested by Sandy's parents and their friends, only to find out later that it is illegal in Oregon to have that particular brew in our possession. If caught, it would carry a stiff fine plus loss of beverage. No arrests were made.

By this time, we were getting tired and anxious to get home. Mona has seats that make into a bed. Since traveling through the Mt. Shasta area is not too scenic, I lay down in back cautioning the girls not to exceed the speed limit, which they both had the tendency to do on straight, flat highways. I lightly dozed only to come wide awake when I heard them giggling and seeing the trees flying past at hurricane speed. "We're not going over 70." they claimed, but I knew better. They admitted later that they were going 90.

Home at last. Back to school for all three. I did come home to find that brother, Keith, had fallen at the mill breaking both legs and hands. I have spent quite some time with him in the hospital and at home. He has had a long convalescence, but has healed well and soon will be back to work.

Hopefully you are still awake after reading this drivel.

May this holiday season bring you choice blessings and at least one good thought.

Love, Shirley, traveler

CHRISTMAS 1978

Dear Family and Friends,

This year didn't start out on a happy note. In January, my sister, Melna, died suddenly of a heart attack leaving a void in all of our lives, especially my brothers, whom she has always spoiled when around. I remember once when I was about eight years old; she came home from California where she was living at the time. Even though she was not a hair stylist, by the time she left, I was the only one without a crew cut. My brothers were the envy of all their friends as that style of hair was not quite 'in' in our area.

In June, Sandy left for "greener" pastures. She was through at LCC and in the fall headed for Western Washington University where she is majoring in education. We all miss her lively, efficient self.

When Sandy moved out, the Bonds moved in. They were building a new house, and the old one sold sooner than they thought it would, so they needed a home. Poor things, they were stuck with me. It was somewhat crowded. The old folks in the extra bedroom, Tim in the back room which had beforehand served as a storeroom but worked out fine with their bed installed, and the girls on my fold-out couch in the living room. It was a busy household with six extra people in the house usually going six different directions at six different times.

Rose did manage to keep her sanity while building one house, trying to keep this one in order, taking care of sheep, garden and swimming pool belonging to some vacationing friends and chauffeuring all of us hither and yon. She also played nurse for me after a needed surgery. When I went in for my first post surgery doctor visit, he managed to get us to giggle when he asked if I wanted the missing parts put back. No way. I told him I felt like a new person, but asked if he could do something about making me look like one. He informed me he only worked on the bottom end, and he was afraid of what my face would look like if he started working on it. Well, I have been called 'butt face' at times.

In August, the Bonds moved into their new home and my new helper, Pam, moved in. Even though she is a happy person who loves to tease, it still seems utterly quiet around here.

Pam is a seventeen-year-old with the usual teen-age malady... boyfriend troubles. She seems to have one boy crisis after the other.

Job wise, I am down to 28 students from the 43 of last year, lessening some paper work. Of course, I still have days when I feel like winding some of them up into my spokes.

Fires seem to be my nemesis. First it was Rose's field, then my chair, now this time it was my classroom. I received a new overhead projector, plugged it in and went to help a student when several students yelled "fire." I turned to see smoke billowing toward the ceiling from the new machine. I had forgotten to remove some unnoticed inside packing. A student had by then unplugged it, but not soon enough to keep the smoke from filtering through the ventilation system throughout the building. Needless to say, a few teachers and the principal were a little excited as each thought it was in their area. I hope this doesn't mean I'll move on to "bigger-n-better" fires in the future.

In October, Rose and I toured the King Tut exposition in Seattle. We are supposed to be far advanced from the Egyptian civilization, but not so artistically, for when you view the craftsmanship of 3000 years ago, nothing we have now seems to be any more beautiful.

My latest adventure was our power outage over Thanksgiving. I didn't realize how much I relied on electricity until I couldn't use my electric toothbrush, move my powered bed up or down, or turn on my heating pad or electric blanket. A friend rescued me and took me to his house with a fireplace. He did chuckle a bit when he found me in bed fully clothed, plus hat, coat and fur-lined boots. Their half-cooked turkey was finished on the BBQ along with potatoes roasted in coals and cold rolls.... A Pilgrim sort of TG.

Now off to an adventurous 1979.

God bless and Merry Christmas.

Love, Shirley, arsonist

Toledo High School Faculty & Staff.
I'm the one in the wheelchair :)

CHRISTMAS 1979

Hi to All,

We here in the northwest were blessed, and I do mean BLESSED, to have in January and February the driest and sunniest months for the last 17 years. (Usually I had to drag out of bed hating to go out into the dark drizzle where I had to force myself to smile and say, "Good morning" to my students when I knew it was not a GOOD MORNING.)

In March, it became evident with power failures at inopportune times and parts falling off, littering the planet, that I would have to purchase a new w/c or get up and walk which would take too much effort after sitting for 24 years. A new one was ordered with the promise it would be delivered in May. In the meantime 'Old Bertha' gave up completely making it necessary to regress to my old, reliable pushchair. I had forgotten how independent power had made me. The new model with its bigger wheels and tires looks more like I am outfitted for plowing; however, I wouldn't have cared if it looked like a Mac truck as long as it moved under its own power.

In the spring, my principal decided I needed a change in teaching assignments. Was it because I became incoherent at times and was morphing into a dysfunctional person myself? I am teaching three classes of Washington State History, two of advanced vocabulary and one of careers. The latter three are composed of junior and seniors. It is rather fun to teach some bright kids for a change.

The summer was spent having outings with the Bonds, a few trips to Portland to visit relatives, and a couple of ventures to the beach.

One day, Rose and Son were visiting when Rose announced she needed to run an errand. Son and I were playing cribbage on my patio when a darn bird decided to drop his doo doo right on my bare shoulder. That darn Sonny just laughed and refused to wipe it off. You can imagine how crusted it was by the time Rose returned an hour later. Somehow, I'll get revenge.

At the beginning of each school year, in order to make the kids comfortable around this woman who always sits and uses a funny contraption to write with, I explain what happened to me. Usually when I ask them if they have any questions, they ask simple ones like "How do you get into bed? Can you drive a car?" etc. But one kid this year asked a question that almost undid me. Our conversation:

Me. "Since my spinal cord was severed, I can't voluntarily move or feel from my shoulders."

Kelly. "You mean if I hit you, you wouldn't feel it?"

Me. "No."

Kelly. "If I cut you, you wouldn't feel it?"

Me. "No, I wouldn't."

Kelly. "Would you bleed?"

Suppressing a laugh and wanting to say, "No I am a vampire," I explained that I would bleed and the rest of my organs worked normally, also.

One beautiful spring day, I decided to enjoy the sun and wheel home as I sometimes do rather than call Pam to come retrieve me. Big mistake this time. I had had my shoes removed after school as my feet were swelling. Since I wear nylons, my feet were somewhat slippery and with each little bump I traversed, they would slide a little further off my foot rests until they were completely off pulling me forward from my chair. By the time I got to the bottom of the hill, I was lying, rather than sitting in my chair. With each passing car, I got more curious looks, and I become jitterier knowing that the next bump might find me with my "butt" on the pavement. Luckily, a neighbor's little boy came by, and with a sigh of relief, I asked him to get his mom. She was frightened as he had just told her I needed help, but she cracked up laughing (I'm sure I was quite a sight), yanked me up, and I have not wheeled anywhere again without shoes.

I have tickets for Pam and me to spend Christmas with my family in Pocatello. I am anticipating a Christmas filled with kids, noise, food and merriment. I haven't had a C. like that in a long time.

Joy to all,

Love,

Shirley, dragging lady

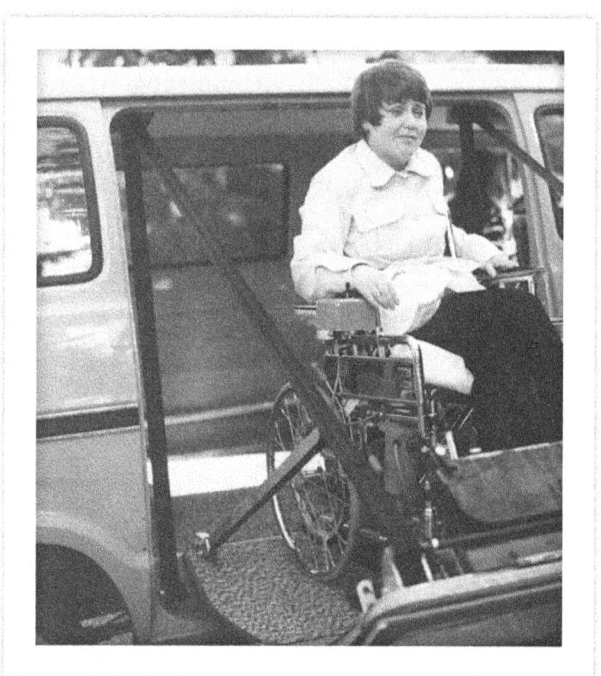

"Mona," my trusty van...

CHRISTMAS 1980

Greetings from Ashville,

Find a comfy place to sit for this year's tale is long but, hopefully, entertaining.

As most of you know the eruption of Mt. St. Helens located close to us has been an experience I never want to see repeated. Although we in Toledo received no damage from the flooding, we did get four inches of ash plunked into our little town. Since she continues to burp at times, we pray the wind is blowing away from us. Every able-bodied person was inducted into cleanup crews, sweeping off roofs, aiding, feeding and providing housing for search parties. (87 people lost their lives.) Son Bond's brother-in-law and five other Toledo acquaintances have not been found. In June, I was able to fly over the area and the devastation is overwhelming. Hopefully, we have seen the last blasts from Heaving Helen.

The ash not only made a mess, it also caused me some mechanical situations I don't care to repeat. I had a dental appointment which fell on the day after the second eruption, and even though school was canceled for the year and my dear principal told me to stay home rather than help, as the teachers were required to care for the National Guard search crews who were lodging at the school (I am sure he thought I'd be more of a hindrance than help). I knew I'd have to keep the appointment, as they are as hard to get as it has been to get the hostages out of Iran. A drive that usually takes 15 minutes took Pam and me over a half hour. The ash is unique. When wet it is as heavy as cement; when dry it blows around in huge clouds making visibility almost nil. I began to unload from the van and was half way out on the ramp door when it took on a mind of its own and went into reverse throwing me upside down onto my back inside the van. Then it began to think it was an express elevator with pauses only on the top and bottom floors, up and down, up and down. Pam was frantically pushing the control button to no avail. While lying there, I remembered I had heard on the T.V. that the ash was causing many electrical shortages and realized that was what was happening here. I had her blow into the controls, and I wasn't sure which was going to expire first, Pam or the lift. The lift finally stopped, I was uprighted. I survived the head bump and the dentist chair. To make sure it didn't happen again, we put duct tape over the outside control. Add that one to your list of duct tape uses!

Later that day, I was out with Pam holding the hose while she was trying to shovel that dern ash from the sidewalk and driveway when my chair leaped forward, turned in circles, zipped across the street, hit a light pole and headed for the neighbor's porch. I was desperately trying to turn it off while holding on and screeching like a barn owl as I surely didn't want to end up being the neighbor's welcome mat. During all of this, Pam kept sweeping away while laughing, as she thought I was just fooling around. Finally, my neighbor, Diane, ran out to see what the commotion was, and yelled for her husband, Dan, who threw my gears into neutral. There I was with my wheels still spinning, but at least I wasn't moving. He pushed me into the house, took my control apart, cleaned out the ash, and I was once again under controlled motion. Needless to say, I stayed housebound until I left SW Washington for a much-needed vacation.

Vacation?? Did I say vacation? More like a test of forbearance. Get ready for a long saga.

Before leaving, Pam had resigned and Paula came to be my Girl Friday. We enlisted Sandy once again to help drive, and after having a mechanic check over Mona and getting a "high five" off we went.

We got a late start but managed to get to Tacoma where we were to spend the night with my college friend, Linda Green and her two chillins. "Don't get out. We are going to Bremerton to have dinner on the 'bay' with my parents," she yelled. As I went to get out at the restaurant, the lift stuck midpoint, leaving me sitting there in midair. Girls retrieved lift instructions from van and started laughing. "It says: if all else fails, to hit the motor with a hammer." It worked! We had a great dinner, but then had to repeat the performance to enter and exit. We left at 8:00 a.m. heading north, then east over North Cascades Pass. We stopped in Newhalem for lunch, but when we tried the hammer maneuver, it refused to budge. I wheeled, and they drove to a service station where a fellow finally managed to get it down and back up, with the advice that I'd best get a mechanic to fix it. I was imprisoned for the rest of the day. We hoped to find a mechanic in Winthrop, a tiny town, which has kept its old west look. The only mechanic there wouldn't touch it. Darn, this was one of my "must see" stops. I did get to see the storefronts; the girls saw the insides.

We had intended to get to Spokane on this day, but with the lift crisis, decided to go to Coulee City where a former student lived who was a good handyman to see if he could retrofit it. He found the problem, something to do with brushes, fixed it temporarily, but said it would need to be replaced somewhere along the way. We spent the night in a little cabin on some very uncomfortable bunk beds.

In Spokane, we spent two days with my niece, Penny, and hubby, Bob. They work at a Catholic retreat, Bob as caretaker, Penny as housekeeper for two priests, and she also takes care of linens for visiting groups. The next day, they had off which gave us an opportunity to scale Mt. Spokane. "I'll sit in the van and read while you guys hike," I said. "No way," Bob said, "You are going." I'm sure he later regretted the idea as the path looked like part of a journey for some former explorer. We high-centered the chair twice on boulders that I couldn't get around and slid half way down on descent. But the view was worth it.

Are you bored yet? If not, read on. If you are, read on anyway. It gets worse.

We stopped to see another college friend. She'd moved to AZ.

Paula drove us through northern Idaho and Glacier National Park as Sandy had a bad case of the flu or had eaten defective vittles. The next day Sandy had revived. We were disappointed in Yellowstone. There were no bears and Old Faithful gave us the impression of a steaming teakettle after our experience with St. Helens. In a good time, the girls' faith was restored in Jackson Hole. From an Alpine slide down a mountain for the girls, we took in a movie set filming "Every Which Way You Can" with Clint baby, watched a "shootout," and headed for the local playhouse to see a rendition of "Calamity Jane." To enter; however, I was faced with a flight of stairs. "Not to worry," some boys said as they hoisted me up. It was during the play that we realized my supermen were some of the actors. They even returned there for the descent.

We left Jackson and headed toward Denver. It was hot, dirty and windy AND, damn, the A/C was out. We spotted a motel out in the middle of Wyoming with sprinklers on. We ate lunch in the shade and I sat in the sprinkler. Then the girls started to laugh. Thinking it was because my hair was plastered to my head, I said that at least I had cooled off. However, they informed me it was because I had a black eye. I had had to take out my contacts (damn dirt) and had rubbed my eye so hard I had broken a blood vessel. We tried to leave the ramp door open a crack for air, but the wind kept blowing it shut, so they kept dumping water on me to keep me from passing out, which I tend to do when overheated. We were glad to get out of Wyoming. At best, we didn't have to try dodging or running over jackrabbits and squirrels.

After 14 hours of driving, we landed at my sister's. I must have been a sight as the neighbor asked, "What happened to you?" We collapsed in bed.

While Mona was hauled away to get both lift and A/C rejuvenated, the girls sunbathed and I read, Gwenie being at work.

Lapboard? Missing? Last seen at that motel in the middle of nowhere. Going back for it? No way. Send for it? Don't know the name of establishment. Make do without it. When I got back to school, I had the shop teacher make me another which is nicer anyway.

I visited with the neighbors that I have known since I was a kid as I had spent a summer with Gwen and Jim at age 11. Bad news, Mona's lift needed a new motor. We extended our visit for two days, borrowed Gwenie's car, site visited, went to amusement park and lounged. Jeff, the hunk of mechanic, brought Mona back, told us he had cleaned out the vents which were filled with ash (so that was where the dirt came from that we blamed on WY) and paid him. We gave him a vial of ash and some pictures of the eruption. You'd have thought we had given him emeralds.

Along our route, we visited the A.F. Academy and Royal Gorge, Four Corners, Grand Canyon. and blessed Jeff every hour for "air."

Six miles out of Kanab, Utah, Mona started heating up. A man stopped to help; diagnosis, bad soft plug, whatever that was. We sat there for an hour, and it still wasn't cooled off. Another guy stopped heading for Kanab. We asked him to send a tow truck. Because it was so late at night, he said he would leave a note on their door. We slept in the van. The next morning, we waited for tow, but there was "no show." Paula poured some water we had melted from the cooler ice and drove back to town. The mechanic couldn't find the problem at the first stop. He sent us to a man who "knew everything" about cars, with Mona clanking to the tune of The Monster Mash, and I was beginning to believe that monster was out to get me. He surmised dirt in fuel line, no, that wasn't it, thermostat? He was the slowest man on this side of the Atlantic. We were thinking we were in Mayberry, R.F.D. But fix it, he did.

We toured Vegas, gambled our $20, took in a show, ate, relaxed and slept.

At seven the next morning, we headed for Lake Elsinor, CA to visit Paula's Hungarian grandparents with a stop in Banning to gab with a couple of step-nieces. Paula couldn't remember the way to our destination. After several tries we finally found someone who could direct us. We arrived. Loved the grandparents, plus their trees with fresh oranges, lemons and grapefruit. We had fresh-squeezed juice every meal. The grapefruit was so sweet you would swear it was a white orange.

"Take a picture of your grandparents." I requested. No camera. We then remembered where it was last seen. Paula had put it in a drawer in our Vegas hotel room. She called. They said they had it, and they would send it to where we would be staying in Middletown. It was hot, hot, hot, 110°. We decided to wait until evening to go to Disneyland's 25th anniversary, where we would get free gifts, and fun.

We took a day of rest then started out for San Diego to see Evelyn, my former German aide whose father was Hitler's architect. We visited Lawrence Welk's restaurant for lunch on the way.

We arrived in San Diego and were going to call Ev for directions. What? We had no address book with her phone number and street address. It was last seen at some service station along the way. Luckily, I did remember her street's name and after crossing a canyon several times, we found the street, but we had no idea what the number of her house was. After driving up and down the street several times, Ev happened to see us. Her apartment is set up like a Japanese home. She sits on the floor to eat, a little problem for me so I balanced my plate on my lap. Ev is also a health freak. We dined on some very weird food. She sleeps on a mat on the floor. Now that was a BIG problem, not only for me sleeping there, but dressing me would also be difficult. Sandy and I decided to sleep in the van.

Up early, we traveled to San Diego Zoo's wild animal farm. We had a lot of fun there with their bird and dog shows, the tram ride, and the walking tour where the gorilla and I had a friendly chat.

On the ride back, I happened to notice the gas gauge said "empty." We couldn't find an open station at 11:00 p.m. I could see us all thumbing a ride. Their theory was to put Shirley out there as all people feel sorry for us who reside in w/c's. We finally found an open station that we coasted into on fumes.

We were up early on Sunday to go to the beach, visit Old Town, and go to dinner at an authentic Mexican restaurant where we saw a fellow upchucking in the bushes. I wasn't sure I wanted to eat there. Ev ordered us margaritas which are served in one hand, 1-1/2-hand and two-hand glasses. That fellow must have had several of the two-handed ones, or maybe like me, can't drink much. By the time we left there, I wasn't worrying about where I was sleeping that night. I rolled out of my chair onto the van bed. I didn't even bother to undress. Ev did neglect to tell me that the men who drove the telephone company trucks that were parked in the alley along side of us, blocking my exit door, came at six to head off to work. As my luck goes, one of the trucks had a flat, so we (Ev slept in the van with me that night) had to wait until that was taken care of before we could exit. Despite all of that, as Ev was leaving... in nightgown, no robe...she slipped on my ramp and ended bottom side up. A good laugh is a great way to start the day.

We paid a day visit to Coronado Beach Hotel where the girls swam in their pool...and Paula got her watch stolen... we had lunch and drinks. We just acted like we were four of their rich guests. Back at Ev's, she cut Sandy's and my hair, and we had cheese and pastry for dinner.

We arose at five so we could miss the telephone men, and the L.A. going-to-work traffic, said our goodbyes and off we went. Twenty miles up the hiway, Mona was yelling, "I'm out of oil." We stopped at a station, where as fast as they put in oil, it went out. The soft plug had blown again. One hour later, we were on the road once more just in time for the L.A. traffic jams.

Stopping in the Danish town of Solvang for lunch, we visited the lovely horse-breeding farms, and spent the night in Monterey. We were very tired and decided we would stay there another day and just relax. The girls sunbathed while I read and people-watched.

San Francisco here we come. As we drove towards town, Sandy began to fume as some guy tried to pick her up at each stoplight we came to. We got on a one-way street going the wrong way, had lunch at Fisherman's Wharf, where the girls were propositioned twice more, but not me, no one was that desperate. To get away from the guys who were following us, they started running, leaving me to my own devices. Just as they were about two blocks ahead, my wheel got caught in a trolley track. I was petrified, as could imagine myself being the next trolley's #1 target. The guys who had been pestering the girls were my Sir Walter Raleighs. They told me they were just having fun with the gals, no danger. That night the girls went to the famous female impersonator club, unavailable to me, those darn architectural barriers... stairs. I lay in bed and watched T.V., while they were off having fun, boo hoo.

We had lunch at Macy's the next day, where we bought fresh-baked bagels and sundry items.

We crossed the bay to Oakland to visit the Jack London Tavern where he had done most of his writing. The bartender watches for new patrons using the restroom facilities and then makes funny remarks that seem to come from the toilets. Upon their return from that area, the girls' eyes were bugging out of their faces. I had my laugh for the day.

At Santa Rosa we bought some cream cheese and Pepsi, and then went to a park to eat our bagels.......... no bagels. Sandy remembered leaving the sack with our purchases on a ledge by the van as we loaded up and, yup, left them there. We called; they had found them. Sandy told them to keep the bagels, send rest to my home address C.O.D. When the package came at home, they had sent everything including by then, the very hard bagels and not COD... nice of them.

Later, we drove over the mountains to Middletown to my friends, Donna and John Monday's, visited with their German exchange students, went to Napa Valley, visited several wineries, had lunch in a park, and went back to Middletown's hill country to see California's hydro-thermo wells.

We left the Monday's and drove as far as Crescent City. We found a nice-looking motel, got undressed for bed, but, alas, found a dirty tissue in my bed. The faucets leaked, and the floor was gritty, yuk, yuk. Sandy called for housekeeping, but the maid made the excuse for the room not being clean as being due to too many guests and not enough help. Bless Sandy and Paula, they insisted we get the room free for our inconvenience, but the motel clerk and the girls agreed to 1/2 off.

Up the coast to Florence we went, to spend a day with my brother, Dan, and his family. They are always good for some laughs, mainly at Dan's expense. After all, he was my childhood tormentor. Some of his antics were as follows: winding my hair into an egg-beater, rubbing cockleburs into my golden locks, helping me far up into a tree and leaving me there, but the worst was stamping my face, arms and legs with an indelible ink stamp, which left "H. F. Stinger" on said body parts until my skin sloughed off.

Finally we were homeward bound. After 26 days on the road, my little duplex looked like Heaven. We were exhausted. And I bet you are, too, after reading this tale.

Despite all of our van and lost item problems, we had a fun-filled, memorable trip.

Back to school and end of saga.

Loves and Merry Christmas.

Wheels, as my students have nicknamed me

P.S. I had borrowed a 35mm camera to get slide pictures of all the county court houses we saw along the way for my Washington State History students to view, but as usual with my luck, when I retuned home, the film was all blank.

Vancouver, B.C. or bust!

CHRISTMAS 1981

Greetings From God's Country,

My nephew, Don, once told me, yes, it is God's country as He is the only one who would have it, and that was about true for this past year.

Because of Mt. St. Helen's burping last year, we still have ash dropping out of trees and other places that neither man nor nature cleared away. My lawn needs to be roto-tilled so the ash will mix in with the soil. The grass just won't grow with "wet cement" on top.

In February, Roxann, Rose's daughter, and I were playing cards at the dining room table when the chandelier started swinging, table jiggling, and dishes clattering in the cupboards. I realized we were having an earthquake. It was over before I could say that that was what was happening. Roxann's statement was, "That's all? I want it to do it again."

Just recently we had what was deemed a hurricane, which we never have here. It did little damage at my house, but many lost trees, barn roofs and shingles from their homes, but the biggest loss was eight lives throughout SW Wash.

We had such warm weather in January and February that we had to mow what lawn was growing.

The Spanish class had a raffle in the spring, the prize being a three-minute shopping spree at a local market. I sacrificed my dollar, and for the first time in my life and probably the last, I won. My young friend, Kay, and I scoped out the joint, decided what would be best to grab; and then as they timed her, she scooped up $186 of groceries. Other than perishables, I haven't had to buy groceries yet.

In July, even though I had quite bald tires, a couple of my former girls and I visited Vancouver and Victoria B.C. Believe it or not, no problems other than the girls getting seasick on the ferry ride... quite rough water causing the boat to pitch at a 45° angle. I guess because I am in motion most of the time in my chair, I didn't succumb to the potty bowl as they had to.

Some friends, Tami and Tom Knickerbocker, invited Shirley (still my weekend help) and me to dinner at the apartment complex they manage in Tacoma. We had just finished our meal when a tenant ran in to tell Tom that a female tenant seemed to be in trouble as she was screaming. He was right about the screaming. When Tom opened the door, you'd have thought a flock of banshees had attacked. Tom and Tami ran to her rescue only to be taken hostage along with another couple she had already threatened. Neither Shirley nor I knew what to do other than make sure Tami's baby was taken care of. Someone called the police and they in turn called mental health. Legally, they said they could do nothing unless she actually shot or harmed one of them. After four hours of haggling back and forth, they subdued the 280 lb. naked woman and took her to the hospital. We all got some laughs out of the ordeal as during the "hostage crisis," she kept propositioning Tom saying she would let the rest go if he would accept her sexual advances. I can't recall all of the other strange things she said and did, but do remember that she told Tami she didn't deserve such a "hunk" of a man.

Mona finally gave up and died. I now have what the kids have dubbed "The Blue Whale." Shirley said it was appropriate for me as it is handicapped blue.

School goes well even though I get harassed by the male teachers. I can give it right back, though. One of our coaches managed to get his team into the state playoffs. I bought him as big of a jock strap as I could find, presenting it to him in the teacher's lunchroom, telling him it was for support while at state. He held it up and exclaimed, "Wow, Shirley, how did you know what size to get?" "Remember, I was once your baby sitter," I replied.

At this time, I feel my age. While in the grocery store, I overheard a mother tell her child not to stare at the "woman" in the w/c. I'm deflated. I am no longer the "girl" in the w/c.

Many blessings to all in the New Year.....

Love, Shirley

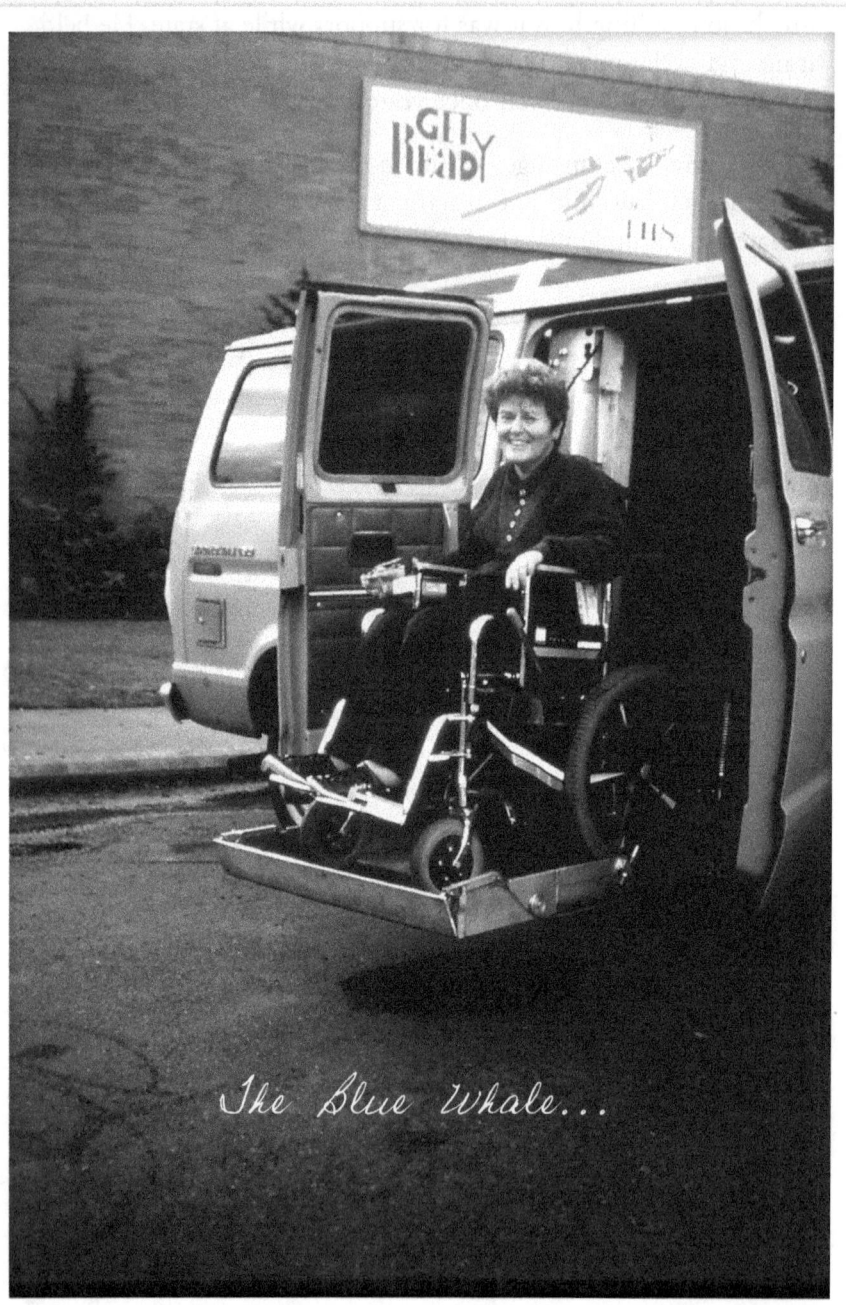

The Blue Whale...

CHRISTMAS 1982

Holiday Greetings,

I have a new teaching assignment this year. Senior Math. A course all students must pass to graduate. It consists of students who do not have high math capabilities. Most of the kids take it seriously, but I do have concerns for three football players. I give a test every two weeks to check their progress. On one such day, these three did not show up, although I knew they were in school. After class, I located them in the gym and ordered them to the classroom. I informed them that they would be receiving a failing grade for this test. Two of them apologized, but the third, who happened to be the star football player, began to argue, as he knew this would make him ineligible for a big game that week. I refused to give in. As he left the room he yelled back to me, "You can take your f... ing test and shove it up your a..." To the principal's office I went. Later that evening, we had a parent conference with not only the parents, but also with the football coach. I have great respect for John, the coach, for even though it might mean a loss of a district playoff game, he told the parents that their son would not be playing. And yes, they won the game without him.

In July, a teacher friend (Allison), Roxann and her friend, Kim Anderson, plus my newest slave, Barbara, headed out on a trip through most of the western states. Our first stop was Boise to visit Dale's family. Rox and Barbara said to save having to get two motel rooms that they would sleep in the Blue Whale. Little did I know...those two (Kim chose not to join them) had other plans than sleeping. Boys! They had seen some while we were checking in. This happened again in San Antonio when they sneaked off

Me & Tanya

My neice Darlene & girls, plus my Uncle Jay Stinger in Salt Lake City, Utah

to a movie with others of the male gender. This time they were caught by ME. Dangerous? No comprende. By the time we got to AZ, those two had been such brats that instead of going on to Disneyland and San Diego, we just headed home. They even ate my candied almonds that I had bought as a gift for a friend.

Since that trip had been such a disappointment, my friend, Jo, her mother and I left to spend a week in San Francisco. Since Jo had once lived in the SF suburbs, she could squire us around without the fear of me getting lost again. We pulled into a nice-looking motel within walking/wheeling distance of Fisherman's Wharf. As we were unloading, we noticed some men exchanging some strong words in another language, which we thought might be Spanish. We tried to ignore them as we wended our way to our room. However, the argument continued in the room above us, and as Jo set about depositing me on a bed, it appeared to get louder and louder. Then bam, gunshots. Jo immediately told me not to move, like I was capable of it, while she frantically tried to call the desk. No one would answer the phone. She finally got the operator who called the police, but while this was going on, there were more shots, and she was yelling to her mom and me to either get under the bed or into the bathroom. Now really, was I supposed to sprout wings? Being frightened, she had suddenly made me "normal" in her mind. We did not find the result of the police action (other than seeing some hauled off via police car and some by ambulance) until the next morning. Jo could not believe the nonchalant attitude of the manager who merely said, "We are used to this. We get these Arab drug traffickers all the time." We moved to another motel for the rest of our stay.

As all must know, SF has steep hills to traverse no matter where you go. Such was the case as we headed down to the wharf. My chair, when faced with a steep grade, tends to slide if I don't go full speed. I neglected to inform my companions of this fact as I took off. As I neared the bottom of the hill, I spied a throng of people pointing to something behind me while at the same time they were jumping to one side. I landed on a flat spot, whirled around to see what the commotion was, only to see Jo and her mom running and yelling about a runaway w/c. I knew I had control; they didn't. Moreover, they didn't appreciate my laughter one iota.

The wharf was fun. We passed on the excursion boat to Alcatraz and headed to Chinatown. As I wheeled along the sidewalk, the Asians would come up to me, feeling and checking out my chair while asking me questions in Chinese. How was I to know what to answer? I dunno Chinese. I just giggled and let them poke around. It was a new experience. You'd never see a Caucasian doing this. They try to ignore me, as I'm sure they think they would hurt my feelings. I'd rather they ask as little kids do, that is, before their parents drag them away.

Remember, I am an oddity. Most w/c bound people are either kept at home or are in nursing homes. We are not supposed to be out in public. That reminds me of how uninformed the public is. I can't tell you how many times I have been shopping for some item, and the clerk says to whomever is with me, "What is SHE looking for?" I just tell the girls to answer with, "I don't know, ask her." I guess they think we in mobile chairs are mentally retarded.

In September, I got new weekend help, Wendy C. She was doing great until she had to give me my first enema. Although she was quite nervous, she managed the procedure. She started to say something to me but all that came out was "ugh" as she fell across my face. She had fainted. What to do? I couldn't breathe, couldn't move her and when I had about passed out myself, she slid onto the floor. I was beside myself, as could not reach a telephone to call for help. As in most cases of emergencies, it seemed like forever before she aroused, but actually it was just a few minutes. I wasn't sure she was going to be able to handle the job, but as of now, she has done fine. We've had some good laughs at her expense.

Each year, Jo has me come to her third grade class to explain why I am in a w/c, and then we open it up to questions. They can come up with some doozies. I also let them go outside and see how my van works. One parent told me when he saw me at a game, that his little boy kept insisting that they get a "car" like Mrs. Watson's as "it has an elevator and you can even sleep in it." My life is never dull.

Watch for the Blue Whale on Trapper John. They were filming an episode as we were driving down Lombard Street in SF.

Happy Holidays,

Love from me, the object of your affection and others' curiosity.

Shirley

CHRISTMAS 1983

Greetings From Bedlam,

Although I constantly live in a state of confusion, I do have my moments of sanity. However, the following excerpts from this past year contain none of the latter.

In February, I made an excursion to Mt. Rainier with the high school's Alpine Club. My purpose... to give them lessons in weight lifting, first aid, and experiencing the tribulations of a day in the life of a handicapped person trying to act "normal". My friend, Chuck, who is the leader and mentor of their expeditions, insisted on me going after I had made several comments on how much fun they seemed to have on their hikes, ski trips, etc. But I was reluctant to go even though I, in my able-bodied days, had enjoyed such outings. My first reluctance, I was positive they would tire quickly from packing me uphill; second, my sensitivity to cold; and third, I did not want to give Chuck any more responsibility than he already had. He assured me that he had all of the clothing I would need to keep warm and claimed he had previously carried heavier loads than I would be. Therefore at 6:00 a.m. we, five adults and eleven students, started off... me looking like a wiener in a large bun rather than a human in a ski suit. Attire: three pairs of socks, woolen underwear, two sweaters, ski pants, jacket, woolen hat and scarf. When we arrived at our destination, the first chore was to cut foot and handholds in the bank; then Chuck and a student took turns packing me up a long steep incline and then on a nice jaunt to a suitable place where they planned to build their igloos. As they cut blocks of packed snow, I watched and "supervised." About this time, ole Sol decided to join us with the result of me having to shed some of my glamorous wardrobe. Amid periods of hard work and laughter, they finally had erected four igloos. One was deemed suitable for some of them to stay in overnight, but I wasn't going to be one of those frozen popsicles. A couple of us bid adieu, slid back down the bank and headed home. No cuts, scrapes or bruises. Having made that big statement aloud, wouldn't you know, as I came in my front door, I caught my foot on the doorframe and sprained my ankle. There I was, the most protected among the group and the only causality had to be at home at the end of the journey. Now Chuck has plans to build an all-terrain wheelchair so that I can go on hikes with them this coming spring.

A month later, Rose and I took Roxann and some of her friends skiing at White Pass. No big bundling job this time. Rose and I stayed in the lodge, visited and read in front of the fireplace while sipping on hot chocolate. Before we were due to leave, Rox brought one of the boys in with blood all over his front. He had fallen while checking out some cute lass skiing next to him. The first aid team pronounced that he would live, did not need transporting, but might be checked out for a broken nose. For once, I was not the victim.

When school was out, Rose, her daughter Shirley, her sister Barbara and I spent two days at a bed and breakfast on Whidbey Island, compliments of my friend, Jack, who teaches math in the adjoining room to mine and who also has had to protect me from a couple of unruly boys more than once. Some of my students have short fuses and are in need of anger management. Anyway, he said he had paid for lodging for my boyfriend and me. "And just where is this boyfriend?" I asked. His reply was that I had three weeks before departure to find one. I told him I had been looking for one for twenty years, and I didn't think I was going to find one in three weeks. The girls had to fill in. Even though we were met with rain and more rain, there wasn't a shop, road or an ice cream stand on Whidbey that we missed.

Because July was very rainy, I spent my time indoors, sanding,

sanding, applying varnish, sanding again, and brushing more varnish on two doors that my w/c tends to eat up when it gets hungry. I didn't think I was ever going to get them back to my desired finish. I was almost done when the wood shop teacher, Mel, happened to stop by and explained I was using the wrong finish. Plus, he said, "You do not stir any kind of finish." That is why you get those bubbles." After using his advice, getting the correct material, and NOT stirring, I was quite pleased with the outcome.

In August, my nieces, Susan and Kaylene, spent two weeks with their old auntie. I have missed them tremendously since they have moved from the Portland area. We had an overnight stay in Victoria, B.C with its beautiful old Empress Hotel where we had tea and crumpets, saw Butchart Garden's spectacular flower beds and the night light shows, toured the wax museum, and what I consider the best aquarium/museum in the NW. On the way from there we drove up to Hurricane Ridge. From the top, you can see all over the Olympic Mountains, feed popcorn to deer and watch the antics of the marmots.

The girls also took a local flight over Mt. St. Helens so they could see the devastation.

While they were here, another niece was getting married in Portland. This niece is of the Jewish faith, and if you've never been to a Jewish wedding, you have missed a lot of fun. Food, food and more food, lots of dancing and laughter.

Some friends from Texas came to visit in August. As with everyone else who comes this way, they wanted to drive to see where the eruption was. It was a hot day and running the A/C was necessary. At a remote spot where the flood area had cut a large ravine, we stopped, and they hiked around the area while I roasted in the shade of the van. All aboard! The Blue Whale refused to move. Dead battery. I was hot. Once before when I had had Mona, we had started the van by hooking my chair battery and Mona together with jumper cables. We had put the chair on full power and the deed was done. But this time, no worky.

Several cars whizzed by. After about 45 minutes with me dying in the heat, a nice, friendly young man came to our rescue. The next day, I purchased a heavy-duty battery.

Wow, time for my 30th class reunion. We gathered at our local park and feasted on a potluck dinner. We old chums were chatting away, when a young Japanese boy on a bicycle pulled up. It was plain to see that he was traveling as he had a large pack on the back of his bike. We invited him to eat with us, and during the conversation, he asked about accommodations at the park. Restrooms we had but showers, no. I asked him if he wanted to stay at my place, as I had a spare room. He had limited English, but he understood that and quickly took me up on the offer. That young Japanese man was traveling around the whole U.S. He stayed for two days and was a delightful guest. He could read and write English quite well, but as with most foreign language classes, they don't teach you much of the spoken language. For this reason, we mostly communicated by pen and paper. He wrote down my address, and I have already received two postcards from him.

That tale reminds me of a job one of my profs in college gave me. I was paid $5 a session to teach a Chinese girl American idioms. She did not understand why someone would say such things as "jump in the shower," "kick his butt," or "hit the sack." She took all these literally, and it certainly was getting her into some awkward situations. I'd have her write down the ones she heard; then I'd explain. We had some laughable sessions.

I've rattled on long enough. Now I'm going to go "shoot the breeze" with my neighbor.

Love to all,

Shirley

Pat Lowe Beibeau & I being goofy at our class reunion...

Me & Jerry Nolan (Clint Eastwood's double)

Class Reunion

Thirteen members of the Class of 1953 of Toledo High School, and their spouses, met at the Toledo Community Park on Sat., July 23, for a reunion.

There were 32 in the graduating class of 1953.

Traveling the longest distance to attend was Jay Massey, from Pasco, WASH.

Mardell (Allen) Murray organized the reunion and was hostess for the potluck dinner.

The group enjoyed visiting and reminiscing.

During the evening, a 22-year old Japanese man from Kumanoto, Japan, who is touring the U.S. by bicycle, came to the park to pitch his tent for the night. He was invited to eat with the group and entertained them by telling of the experiences he has had so far on his journey. He has been in the for one month, and plans to d a year.

hen he arrived in the U.S., he e only three phrases in lish, however, he spoke gh English at the park to nunicate with those present, ugh gestures were used at

sayuki was invited to spend ight at Shirley Watson's e and invited to spend time at ome of Bernard Johnston and ife, Sandra, in Renton, when rived there.

reported Americans had most kind to him and, so far, d only had to buy food twice, and spend two nights in his tent.

Class members hope this kind of hospitality will continue throughout the remainder of his U.S. tour.

Chuck and students pulling me in custom built Ski Sled

Happy 49th Birthday to me!

CHRISTMAS 1984

Greetings From Cripville,

1984 was a year of firsts for me... my first time on skis and my first broken bone.

Shortly after I mailed last year's letter, my friend, Chuck, told me not to plan anything on my birthday, which falls on Dec. 28th, as he had plans for a fun outing. I called his wife, Sally, to see what his plans were, but she would not divulge his secret. A few days before his big treat (treatment?), he came to my house dragging a strange-looking contraption. It wasn't until he picked me out of my chair and deposited me in it that I realized what he had in mind. It clearly resembled Santa's sled... from the color to the skis but minus the reindeer!! I woke up to a very cold 38° 49th birthday. Soon I was dressed in my reject Army woolies, and Chuck, several students and I headed for the slopes of Mt. Rainier. We arrived, out came the sled, next came me. I informed Chuck that I would need my air-inflated cushion to sit on. As he went to lay it in the sled, I noticed it was curled in half. What the heck was going on? It was not like that at home. Chuck, being a science teacher, explained that the higher elevation was causing the pressure inside the cushion to be greater than that outside of it. Releasing some air corrected the problem. Cushion on seat, me settled on top, and amid stares from the curious, I nervously was ready. I was wondering what this transplanted abominable snowman was getting me into. With Chuck on skis and a rope tied around his waist taking up the front end, student Lonnie pushing from behind and me looking like Nanook of the North, we started the ascension into my, as yet, unknown experience. Those going up and down the mountain stopped statue-like and stared until we were out of their sights. When my "reindeer" got winded, we stopped and ate our lunches. Upward and onward we went until we reached our turn-around spot where the fellows got their 20th wind. Then down the mountain we whooshed. What a reward for being a good girl all year. It was exhilarating. Darn, it was over far too soon. What had taken an hour to trudge up took only 10 minutes to "fly" down. The onlookers laughed when they realized what we were doing. They had previously thought my human deer were rescuing me from some terrible accident. I was able to hit the slopes once more, but an early rainy season, and I'm sure my exhausted comrade, prevented further outings.

Now to the broken leg. NO I did not break it skiing. Coming home from a shopping spree, I had my legs crossed and misjudged the width of a door and caught my foot on the doorframe, yup, again. I am a slow learner. As Bruce, a teaching peer, keeps reminding me, "The slow kids get the slow teachers." Thinking I had just sprained it again, I did not go in for X-rays, and I was not going to miss leaving the next day on a planned trip to Canada. During the trip, I kept perspiring, a sign that I am hurting somewhere, which in turn requires some exploring to find the cause. This time, it did not require a search, as I knew it was the leg. The Canadian Rockies are spectacular, and I tried to enjoy them, but I was getting nauseous. My leg and foot by this time were looking like a giant eggplant. Finally on the eighth day, I agreed to cut the trip short and go home. We stopped in Longview's emergency room. X-ray's showed that both leg bones were broken, had started to mend only not as they should, requiring them to be rebroken, set and put in a cast from toes to thigh. As we stopped at home, Sue, my newest slave, looked as if she had seen Dracula. The look on her face was one of disbelief. Being instructed at the hospital that it was imperative to keep my leg elevated, Rose managed to rig up a board that went below the seat, rested on the battery case, stuck out long enough for my leg to rest on it, and then she tied my leg to the board. Made a great ramrod to "accidentally" subdue naughty students.

Sue is so much fun. Always on the ball and finds humor in my "situations." She was out for the evening, I was in bed watching

T.V., when I began having trouble breathing, and my chest and arm hurt. Heart attack! I called my neighbor, Shirley Grubb; she ran down, called an ambulance, located Sue, and off the three of us went to the hospital. Diagnosis, not a heart attack but pleurisy. A shot, some antibiotics and back home within two hours. Sue says she doesn't dare leave again as she never knows what "mischief" I will get into next.

Prior to the Canadian trip, I went with a couple of teachers to the southbound rest stop on I-5 near Toledo where we dispense free coffee and cookies to weary travelers. Donations are accepted which are used to help fund the science team. It was our duty to put the free coffee sign out a mile down the highway, which we had forgotten to stop and do. To do it by car meant going south to the next exit, then north to another one and back to the rest stop, a distance of ten miles. I don't know what compelled me to offer, but offer I did. I was to wheel along with someone to go back up the freeway to put the sign out. I was warned that it was a long way, but since I had done it on the northbound side, I assured them we would be back in 15 minutes. Along with my friend, Kay, we ventured forth. 15 minutes, ha. Not one mile but two. Why the disparity in distance from northbound to southbound has yet to be explained. By the time we reached our destination, my hand and arm were causing me misery from having to continuously hold onto my joystick, (Why is it called a joystick? Brings no joy to me unless you count that it enables me to move.), and Kay said her thighs hurt for a week. We were amused during our stint from the truckers and other vehicles who honked, waved and gave us thumbs up. I'm sure they thought, since they had not seen a car in trouble parked along the way that we must be hiking through the U.S. for some worthy cause. Eventually, we arrived back at the rest stop. I doubt that that offer will come forth from me again.

1984 is almost at end and so is this letter. May you be blessed with warmth, nourishment and good health in '85.

Love to all,

Shirley, skier/hiker

Aloha! From Hawaii...

CHRISTMAS 1985

Dear Family and Friends,

Again this will be a long one as my Hawaiian trip was filled with perils. I know you are anxious to read about it. Some of you have already heard about it, so you can skip that section, the rest of you get your hanky and read on.

Early in December, my niece, Dell, said she was buying me a ticket to spend Christmas with her in her condo in Hawaii. I was so excited! Warm sun, great view, and lots of good food were printed on my mind. However, this venture would prove to be a test of my forbearance.

I was to travel via a charter flight out of Portland, PDX. I had arranged for a couple of my student musclemen to drive me there and then transfer me from my chair at the entrance of the plane and carry me to my seat. However, I woke up that morning to bitter cold and with warnings that the freeway was covered with black ice. Worrying that the boys had little experience on icy roads, Chuck, once again, came to my rescue. We arrived in plenty of time, and because people who use w/c are loaded first, Chuck got me settled and bid me good-bye. On account of I am so short, my feet would not touch the floor. I knew that before my six-hour flight was over, I would be hurting. Imploring the flight attendant to find something to rest my feet on resulted in receiving two very flat pillows that did not begin to reach my tootsies. Dangle they must. Off we went. After being air born for a while, I was getting cold. NO BLANKETS to be had. Plus the teenager sitting next to me acted as if I had leprosy. Frozen and hurting, we finally landed. I had previously made arrangements with Kelly (son of my friend JoAnn), who was stationed there in the Navy, to meet me and help me from the plane in Honolulu to the inner island flight to Maui. No problem. Oh yuh?

"We can't take a motorized chair on our flights," said the boarding attendant.

"How do you think I got it this far?" I asked. "I just twitched my nose and here it is?"

My hero, Kelly, demanded to see the boarding superior. Not wanting to cause a further scene, they gave me the okay. Twenty minutes later I was in Maui where Dell and Dick met me with a beautiful lei and a van that he had rented. Out from the baggage compartment came my chair; I was deposited into it, but it refused to move. A belt was broken. We decided to deal with that later as Dick pushed me up the ramps into the van.

Because I had been up for 22 hours, I was tired, cold and anxious to go to bed. Arriving at the condo, I groaned. It was upstairs. Dick, not being young, assured me he could carry me up, which he did, but my chair is very heavy and proved to be too much for him. We decided to leave it in the van, and rent a pushchair the next day. A cup of hot tea and on to slumber land.......

The next morning, I was rejuvenated with tea and fresh fruit served on the lanai. A tour of the island was the plan for the day. We had been out only a half hour when the van decided it didn't want to go any further. Called rental for replacement. None were available nor did we have any success with getting a mechanic... no one works over the holidays. A friend of theirs came to rescue us in his car; then off we went to find a w/c shop to rent a pushchair. There was no such place and calls to Honolulu were negative. Through friends of friends, they located one we could borrow. It was a relic---rusty, seat torn, and foot rests six inches below my feet. Before we got back to the condo, my foot had gotten caught in a wheel, resulting in a few slash marks but no broken bones or sprain. Dell wadded up some towels, which provided a resting place for my feet and enabled me to be moved about the house. End of sightseeing.

Christmas day, I agreed to plunk my fanny once again in the dilapidated chair and go to dinner that consisted of Japanese food at a teacher acquaintance's home. Then came wind and rain, and there went my sunbathing. Four days spent playing cards, and it was time to fly homeward.

After arriving at the airport, we were told that the connecting flight was delayed. Kelly was to meet me in Honolulu and get me onto the 5:00 p.m. plane home. After several tries, he could not be located by phone to inform him we were late. At 4:55, and being a rack of nerves, I was finally on the plane. We had been told they would hold the United plane for a 1/2 hr., and it was already past that. Now comes the fun. A young man met me with "my" chair, minus foot rests, arm rests, and batteries, whipped me onto the BAGGAGE CART, amid startled gawkers, me affixed to the back of the chair and wondering how bad it was going to hurt when I was flung onto the concrete. I was conveyed from one end of the tarmac to the other, and hoisted up to the entry of United Flight 402 where a male attendant got me settled into my seat.

Once again, I was confronted with the dangling feet problem; however, this time there were many empty seats. A young couple returning from their honeymoon offered to move over, assisted me in lying down, got me a pillow and blanket, and I was cozy.

We had been in the air about three hours when we were hit with some horrific turbulence; then PLOP went the plane. It felt like we had dropped to the ocean surface; oxygen masks fell, and we were told to buckle up, grab a mask and to prepare for ditching. It was my birthday! I told myself I was brought into this senseless world on this day so I might as well go out on the same. We were all petrified into silence, but for one hysterical lady who was still screaming when the emergency ended. The pilot, forgetting his mike was open to the passenger compartment, had been using some words that I had heard only from loggers. What seemed like 30 minutes was only a minute or so when he explained that the turbulence had shut down the motors; they'd been restarted, so we didn't need to plan our funerals and all was well once more.

Upon landing in Portland, minus w/c parts and also luggage, I was, for once, glad to see rainy, cold weather. It took 10 days and numerous phone calls to every airport involved, to get my belongings back. They were in the storage room in Maui's airport. Dick had been assured three times that no such articles were there. I doubt that I'll ever suggest going to Hawaii again.

A few days after my return, Rose gave me a belated 50th birthday party with all of the black, "over the hill" paraphernalia and gifts, my favorite being a shirt that read, "50 isn't old if you are a tree."

Speaking of shirts reminds me of the time way back when Sandy and Shirley B. were my aides. I had bought the three of us shirts on which I had had printed "Shirley's Slave #1" on Sandy's, "Shirley's Slave #2" on Shirley's, and "I'm Shirley" on mine. We drew some chuckles when we were shopping or traveling. Shortly after that, I noticed they had bought a bullwhip and a sign that said "Slave Quarters" which they had hung on the door of the bedroom that they shared.

Since special ed teachers are hard to find, I have been back teaching that class for a few years. However, in the spring, the principal and I agreed that my-married-with-children teacher's aide had to be let go. She was spending too much class time with one of my senior boys and had even been seen with him in her car on several occasions. I spent the remaining two months without help, but my students were great to fill in as retrievers as I am constantly dropping materials or not able to reach others. Given a little responsibility, they gain confidence in themselves. In the fall, I was granted a new aide, Sherri, who is the wife of our business teacher. She is great and a lot of fun. I am hoping she will stay for a while.

Tired and droopy, I'm off to bed.

Happy New Year to all,

Shirley, slave driver

CHRISTMAS 1986

Dear Friends and Family,

Being the #1 HS basketball devotee, I was kept busy throughout January and into early March going to four basketball games a week. Both our boys and girls have winning teams and since some of the athletes are 'my' kids, I work late in my classroom on home game nights and go right to the gym instead of going home and then back again.

On one such night, it being an away game, I was doing paper work, and waiting for my helper to pick me up at 7:00. It was a Friday night and everyone had vacated the premises. Around 5:00 Satan decided my life has been too serene and banished me into total darkness. When I say darkness, I mean DARKNESS. I could hardly see the pen in my hand. To be in a humongous building by myself in the absence of a glimmer of light is eerie. All I could think of was, "It's two whole hours before help arrives to rescue me." Then from far away, I heard a mysterious sound. "Aha, someone else is in the building after all. I'll try and go for help." Being the brave soul that I am not, I ventured out of my classroom to follow the sound. I know the library well enough that I managed to maneuver through it with only a few bumps into the tables and bookcases, but the long hallway was a different matter. After playing bumper cars with the walls, I headed toward the source of the sound only to find the circuit board had an alarm ringing. Later I was told that the alarm rings to let you know the power is off. I fail to find the logic in that. With the idea that I would feel more comfortable in my room, I reversed my path back only to see headlights coming from around the back of the building where there is no road. Since the school had had a rash of robberies, I just knew someone had decided the blackout was a perfect chance to secure more loot. No way was I going to let them know of my existence in the building. I bulldozed through some desks and hid in a corner away from the windows. The "knock, knock" on the window caused all of my blood to hit my shoes. After several more knocks, I gathered up the courage to yell, "Who is it?" Remembering that I was alone in a dark building, Rose had come to rescue me.

On another late work night, I picked up the phone to call home for my new girl, Brandie, to come get me. Damn, I dropped the portable phone. Then I recalled I had told her to come get me around seven and set about clearing off my desk. 8:00, 9:00, 10:00, and then 11:00. No Brandie. I had read everything within reach. I was bored and tired and was thinking something terrible had happened to her, as she had been so responsible to always be on time. Finally at 11:45, a tearful Brandie ran in. She had fallen asleep on the couch while watching TV, and only when frost settled on her nose did she awaken.

Teachers are constantly having to take classes in order to keep certified, up to date on new methods and also to get raises in pay. I had a long paper due within a week. I had finished writing it in longhand and was ready to type it when I noticed it was missing from my desk. I eye-searched the room, no luck, and then garnered the aid of another teacher, Fran, to hand-search with no results. I decided that some student had needed a notebook, had ripped out the used pages and dumped them into a wastebasket; Fran and the night janitor rummaged through every wastebasket in the building. One never realizes how many wastebaskets a school utilizes until you have to explore them all. Still no papers to be had. The next day, I offered a $25 reward. No takers. I then was forced to call my prof with my pitiful story. "I have listened to some doozy excuses," he replied, "but yours is definitely unique." He gave me a choice; a week's extension or I could drop the class. I was not about to lose the $400 fee the class had cost, so for six hours each night after school, I rewrote and typed as I went. It was an atrocious piece of work, but I got it in on time and passed the class. The mystery of the original paper was never solved.

Over spring break, Rose, Shirley and I went to Seaside, Oregon to relax in the unusual 80° weather. One of those mornings as we breakfasted in a restaurant, we were bombarded with a screaming child at the next table. The parents seemed indifferent to his wailings. I mentioned quietly to my companions that the least they could do was take him out to quiet him down so the rest of us could eat in peace. Later that day, Rose and Shirley were strolling through some shops that had stairs while I found a sunny spot next to a bench. The man sitting there greeted me by saying, "Hello, Shirley." As I turned to see who it was, he laughed and said, "It's me, Gus, with the screaming kid." Gus was a former work-study counselor from my school. I had not recognized him in the restaurant as he had had his back to me. I was embarrassed that he had overheard my remark, but he laughed it off saying he was the one to apologize for his son's bad behavior.

While at home watching TV in July, I heard a loud explosion. I thought someone was belatedly shooting off some fireworks in my yard. I was just about to go investigate when I saw smoke spewing out from the TV. I yelled for Brandie to unplug it, but it just kept smoking. Finally, it burned itself out. I called my neighbor to see what had happened since we didn't have any power anywhere. Apparently a transformer had blown. The PUD was called, power restored, insurance adjuster was called, walls repainted and a check for a new TV arrived. All was back to normal, if you can call my life normal.

Fires seem to cling to me. I have a feeling that that is how I'll meet my end. Going to school one day, Old Blue belched forth a cloud of smoke and died. The wrecker was called. The mechanic reported that it would take several days to fix it. Thankfully, it was nice weather so Brandie and I could walk/wheel to school. I decided to take the shortcut the kids use. Wrong move. The sidewalk is very steep and halfway up my chair lost its power. She released the belts and tried to push me up, but the chair was just too heavy. I had her park me sideways and go for help. She was just out of sight when I started slipping sideways down the walk. I could visualize me landing, smashed on the highway below. By the time she and Chuck came to my rescue, I had slid off the walk and was stopped by a tree. At least I was prevented from being "roadkill."

Still without the van, I stayed one day after school to watch a baseball game. I told Brandie that I would wheel home later. 'Later' found me in the middle of the highway with one clutch slipped off and me going around in circles. Cars drove around me going up the hill. Cars drove around me going down the hill. I yelled and waved. They smiled and waved. Friendly souls. Did they think I was out here playing chicken? Oh, a familiar face, my principal, Dennis. He engaged my clutch and I was once again on my own. I couldn't figure out why he was following me!

That is my list of mishaps for this year.

God bless and may he grant you many blessings,

Love,

Shirley

CHRISTMAS 1987

Greetings from Toledo,

Winter months passed with business as usual. Then in April I was called into the counselor's office only to receive terrible news. Wendy, my former fainting helper, had shot herself. Although she is not fat by any means, Wendy is a tall, big-boned, beautiful girl and felt she would never marry, a thought we all rejected. Since leaving my employ, she had worked at a mill where in an accident, she lost the ends of some fingers, and at that time remarked that she would never get a boyfriend, "As who would want to hold this hand now?" She did, however, have a serious boyfriend who had just broken off their romance. Feeling terribly rejected, she must have thought she would never find happiness. She did survive but has many physical and mental problems that she will have to have help with for a long time. I am still so mad at her. We just cannot figure out why she didn't reach out for help before going to such drastic measures.

The last day of school arrived. I went to the district office to sign some papers. For some reason as I went over the threshold of the office, my chair slipped into high gear causing me to do the wheelie the students are always begging me to do. But I didn't stop at a wheelie; instead, I flipped completely over splitting open my head on the cement. Although I was bleeding profusely, I declined the ambulance they insisted on calling, took the offered towel and wheeled the two blocks to the doctor's office. Five stitches intact, I wheeled on home.

That evening was our annual end-of-school party. I went with Rose and Son, who had his arm in a sling from gout, and Shirley who was limping from an injured ankle. We picked a table and ended up with seatmates, Matt and Jo. She had her arm in a sling, too, as she had tendonitis. Oh well, it provided Rose, Matt and Shirley something to do... cutting up meat, buttering bread and whipping up our baked spuds with all of the trimmings.

The day after the party, Brandie backed Old Blue into the ditch, denting the fender. On that same day while I was at the Bond's, Roxann fixed me a cup of hot water (I don't drink coffee); thought I had a hold of it and let go. I knew I was burned as not only did I start sweating but got a terrific headache. Rose insisted on taking me home and pulled off my jeans along with skin and flesh from my knees to my crotch. Back to the doctor, who proclaimed I had third degree burns. Having been a doctor in Vietnam, he had had considerable experience administering to burned soldiers. He not only debrided them each day, but came to the house to do it.

Against doctor's orders, but assuring him that I had an RN niece, we traveled four days later to Idaho for my family reunion. This was just not going to be an uneventful summer. Usually, I make the trip in one day, but half way there I was feeling rather miserable so found a motel and crashed. Darn chair. The next morning it refused to move its right wheel. I called my brother, Dale, who assured me he would rent a substitute chair, which he did. Apparently the right motor had decided it was going to retire. Because of the burns, I had to wear skirts. Forgetting it had been years since my delicate legs had been exposed to sunlight, I sunburned my legs from knees to shoes. At least the bottoms matched the tops. The w/c was again fixed, but before we could leave town, the left motor of my chair gave up also. Another two days were added to our visit.

The girls have a waterbed in their room, and apparently it decided we weren't keeping the carpet clean enough as Alicia, my weekend help, woke up in the night to a flat bed and a swimming pool for a floor. She called her boyfriend, Lance, who helped to drain the rest. They emptied out my linen closet of towels to soak up the water from the carpet. At 6:00 a.m., I called the landlord, but he was leaving for Yakima and couldn't be "bothered." #$%^&

I finally located a shop-vac, the kids soaked up as much as they could, then Lance decided he could dry it with a hair dryer, oh yeah... "I always finish what I start," he declared after I told him that would take days. Twelve hours later, I convinced him it would dry with the help of fans, which it did. What a dedicated boyfriend.

Brandie became sick and listless. I persuaded her to go to her doctor. "Mono," he announced. "You need two months of bed rest." I frantically looked for new help and found Tammy.

I spent the rest of the summer in and out of the tub having burns scrubbed with a brush. In August, they were healed enough to go back to work and back to pants. For once, I was glad to see summer end. I hoped I would have no more mishaps. Wrong. My chair kept blowing fuses and even the shop teacher couldn't find the cause. I went back to my pushchair and immobility while sending the other to the w/c doc. As my luck goes, it never blew one fuse while he had it for three days. I loaded up on fuses and instructed a student how to replace them.

Later in September, Old Blue started to sound like a 747 taking off. He had to have a new muffler installed.

In October, my chair again refused to move and it wasn't the fuses. My good friend, Jim, the shop teacher, ripped it apart for the umpteenth time. He found that the gears were stripped and ordered $125 of parts through UPS, stressing we needed it FAST. Three days later, they arrived, wrong parts. "We are sorry. We'll send the corrects ones."

"Please send them overnight by Federal Express. We'll send these back with them." I explained that I have a friend who drives this route, and I know he'd see that I would get them.

"Just keep the other parts," the salesman said. Apparently they were not worth the $125 they had quoted!

We waited, waited and waited. No parts. Called Fed Ex. They were delivered three days ago. Where to? Toledo School District office. I called the office.

"Yes, a package came. I just haven't had time to send it up," she explained. Six days of immobility because SHE DID NOT HAVE TIME. You can imagine my thoughts on that subject.

Ross, Hattie, Dan and Vivian (brothers and wives) came for Thanksgiving along with the ones who live here. We ate, ate, laughed and played games.

Luckily, my chair hadn't blown a fuse for a couple of weeks so I felt safe in going to the paper box to retrieve the paper. Not my best decision since Tammy wasn't home. Of course it blew. I yelled for my neighbor, Darrel. Yelled and yelled. No one heard me and no one went by. After twenty minutes of wiggling in my chair with rain streaming down my face, neck and soaking the paper, I succeeded in jolting something back in place and I got POWER. I was inside at last, but there was no reading the limp paper that night. "Was it worth it?" you ask. Apparently not! I threw it in the trash.

Would you believe my neighbor girl, Punky, finally found the source of my fuse problem? She took the control panel off, saw some wires touching, got out the electrical tape, and the problem was fixed. Wouldn't you know it would take a female to fix what the expert MALES couldn't?

Dick and Delores's daughter, Diane, and I left by plane a couple of days before Christmas to spend it with her parents. Looking forward to some warm AZ sun, we had an uneventful trip down. We disembarked to cold 32° weather, which left me returning to Toledo with the same pale face as the one I had left with.

I'm sorry this ended up a short story, but I'm sure you are used to my sorrowful tales by now.

Happy New Year to you and ME.

Love, Shirley, the discombobulated

CHRISTMAS 1988

Hi From Toledo, WASHINGTON

I emphasize WA as we get so confused with either Toledo, OH, or OR. Just last month, I ordered some shoes from a place where I can get small ones. After two weeks waiting for them to come, I called the shoe store. They put a tracer out and found they were in a post office in Toledo, OH even though they definitely had the correct address.

Still being the number one basketball fan, going to games and work kept me busy during January through March, with both boys and girls winning league, district and going on to state.

Our gym does not have a well-situated spot for w/c viewing; therefore, my dear principal, Denny, hefts me out of my motorized chair and transports me up the stairs to the upper deck where I have my push chair. Best seat in the house! On one game night, a fight broke out between one of our players and one from the opposing team. Parents left the stands to break it up; others seeing the commotion joined in. Soon it was mayhem. To quell it, Denny shut off all of the gym lights and ordered everyone out including the players. All complied. I alone was left. After dealing with the police, Denny headed home. There I sat yelling for a while, hoping someone was still there. I had resigned myself to the idea of spending the night in a very dark, deserted gym. It wasn't until he was almost home that he remembered that I was up there. Saved once more.

Both the van and w/c have been making me want to kick and punch them, but decided I can't kick, and punching would only result in bloody knuckles. Both need to be replaced or maybe I need to be. While others can borrow, rent or steal another means of mobility, I cannot. Being without my wheels is like the able-bodied being without their legs. No one gets anywhere. After $1000 in repairs, the chair seems to be perky again, but Old Blue just isn't "cutting the mustard." (I wonder where that saying originated.) The girls and I have decided that if we have to leave our little town, we will enlist a male to ride shotgun, for none of us want to be stranded along the highway waiting for some dude to kidnap us, or is that wishful thinking?

One night in November, Robin, my new girl and also the daughter of my good friend, the shop teacher, was away at a volleyball game while I decided to stay at work and get caught up on such much-needed paper work for the special ed spy who shows up unannounced from time to time. I certainly didn't want to be incarcerated in the sp. ed. cell for noncompliance. Robin showed up around 11:00 and we headed out the door along with her coach. The coach got in her car and left; we got in ours and didn't. Old Blue was being cantankerous and refused to move. No way was I going to call any of my "minute men" at that time of the night. We retrieved the flashlight from its compartment and headed off walking/wheeling into the pitch-black night. Besides the dark, we had fog so thick it would have hidden the beam from the Heceta Beach Lighthouse. AND it was cold. Having no coat on, I convinced Robin to go back with me inside the school, found a kid's sheep lined jacket, and tied a sweatshirt around my head. She grabbed some other kid's coat and off we went. I had to straddle the centerline to avoid ending up in a ditch. Whenever a car would creep up, I would inch to the side of the highway and pray that the drivers would see something and avoid it, but hopefully not recognize it was what "it" was, ME. Two people stopped to offer help, but short of being towed home there was nothing to be done but continue on as before. Because it was so cold, I was going with all jets open down that big hill. As we neared home, we were stopped by the local gendarme. He said he had spotted something flashing by him, but it did not look human nor did it look like any animal he had ever seen. I told him he had never had me in his clutches, or he would know what an animal I could be!

Mary, the mother of one of the BB players, and I went to a non-league game her daughter was playing in at a small college in Portland. Upon leaving, Old Blue once again refused to budge. Mary thought she might check under the hood and as she was so doing, a fellow asked if he could assist us. When we gave an affirmative reply, he then mentioned he would do it for ten bucks. Since we were desperate, I handed over the money. He messed around for a bit, told us to get in the van, start it, and he took off. Yup, you guessed it. It still didn't start. I made an urgent call to AAA. I certainly have received more than my money's worth from them.

In March a new family moved into the other side of the duplex and almost from day one, I prayed that they would soon move. The old guy, whom I later learned was 66, was as ugly as a possum and had a very young wife with two kids by her boyfriend who also "lived with them." During the summer, we found out the kids had the old man's name so he could draw social security for them. Now I know this sounds like some fanciful story made up by some Hollywood screenwriter, but I swear, I doubt that even they could make this TRUE story believable. His 88-year-old mother also lived with them, but we did not know she existed until she escaped one day from the bedroom where they kept her under lock. She ended up on our doorstep, and although she was afraid she'd get us in trouble, we did convince her to come in. After hearing her story, we called the police. He questioned her, called another son who lived in Chehalis, who informed the police he could do nothing as this old guy had her power of attorney and was her designated guardian. The son said he had even gone to court on her behalf to no avail. The horrid son, with whom she was living, was such a con artist that he had even gotten her retirement changed to his name. (I was amazed to find that she had once taught elementary school in Toledo.) Adult protection was called, and showed up the next day, but he claimed he had no mother living there. The court lady got a warrant to search, but to avoid getting caught, each morning he would whisk his mother out of the house and take her somewhere and bring her back late enough when he knew the court representative would be off duty. Robin and I enlisted the help from a couple of her male friends to follow him to see where he was taking her. They got about 15 miles before noticing they were about out of gas and had to return. By this time, the landlord had served eviction papers as no rent had been paid since they had moved there. Do you know how long it takes to evict someone? Six months after serving! The police finally had to literally force them out. I felt so sorry for the mother, but we had done all we could. I still wonder where they went.

In August, I took Robin, her friends, Angela, Teddy and Casey to my brother, Dan's, in Florence, OR, to play on the huge sand dunes there. Borrowing my nephew's 4-wheelers, they took off up and down the dunes. Casey disappeared. We waited and waited but he did not emerge. Thinking he had met some terrible accident, I sent Teddy to look for him. I was about to call search and rescue when they finally materialized. Teddy had located him trying to push the 4-wheeler up a dune. Apparently, he had misjudged the steepness of the incline and ended up nearly buried in the sand. After realizing he wasn't hurt, we cracked up. He was plastered with sand in his hair, ears and nose. A thirty-minute shower finally alleviated that problem. Even though Casey said his ordeal was not enjoyable, they have begged to go back.

My house has become the hangout for Robin and her friends. They spend their time here when not at school, participating in sports or doing homework. They eat and play games, but their favorite pastime is either trying to scare each other or me. In the area, there is a man who has a sign posted on his property that reads "Keep out or be shot." Thinking this was just a way to keep salesmen off his rural property, the kids decided to test his warning. Five pale-faced kids arrived back at my house. He had actually shot at them. They have had other escapades, but have not again been used as targets for a trigger-happy property owner. At least they are not out partying like so many others.

That is it for this year's roundup. Happy Holidays.

Love, Shirley

CHRISTMAS 1989

Dear Family and Friends,

Most of the general population claim that if you want excitement, you need to live in a big city, but in this small town life is never dull, especially not for this physically challenged woman.

January brought an unusual amount of snow. Because school was closed for three days, Robin's friends invaded my "pad" using it as a place to crash between sledding bouts down the middle school hill, which had been blocked off from traffic. They dried clothes, ate and used the living room floor for naps. It was either run over them or be imprisoned either in the kitchen or my bedroom.

I made use of my confinement to enter my taxes into the computer to later print out for the accountant. Just as I was entering December's bills, zap went the power. Snow here is very wet which piles upon trees, roofs and power lines, which caused the line from the street to my house to go down. The PUD was prompt, but my taxes had disappeared into space. Again I tackled the job, but this time I saved each month as I went. Back at school on Monday I retrieved my floppy disk from my backpack to print out my work only to find it was blank. What had happened is anyone's guess. By this time I was ready to tell my taxman to just copy last year's, but since that was not an option, I started over for the third time. You realize it takes considerable time when you type with just one finger. January, save, print, February, save, print until finally the year is on paper and I had a semblance of hair left.

Robin, Me,
Rose & Susan

Jeddy & me on
graduation day

The middle of February brought freezing, icy weather. I was feeling quite smug as I had escaped frozen pipes, had no problem getting Old Blue started and had no latches freezing shut (most of my neighbors had had one or another of these misfortunes). Only to come home to find the young man from next-door trying to fix the faucet in the garage. Although I had had Robin leave the water dripping, it still had frozen, causing water to flood the garage and driveway. I called a plumber, problem solved. A few days later while getting some meat from the freezer, she found the plumber had unplugged it to use his tools and had not replaced it. Recently purchased meat at a cost of $400, and other no-longer edibles, went to the dump rats.

District basketball tourney came next. After leaving the game, I scurried into the dark, rainy night to find my ramp door wouldn't open. Several men tried to find the cause to no avail. They put me in the front seat and a fellow Toledoan put the chair in the back of his pickup. The next day I dressed warmly and wheeled to school while Robin passed me by in my nice warm van. I was sure one of my peers could find the cause and good ole handyman Chuck did. The next week, at a tourney game, it happened again. This time some kind man removed a cotter pin and the door swung free. He tied the door shut and we were homeward bound. We had to use this method for several days while waiting for a new door motor to arrive. While the van was at the shop, I again had to wheel to and from school. Snow was melting, cars went by... splat. By the time I arrived to work, I looked like I had been the winner of a mud-wrestling bout.

In July, my 77-year-old sister, Gwen, who lives in Denver, spent two weeks with me. We went to sites in Seattle, Portland and did the Mt. St. Helen's area tour. However, I don't think she quite understood all of the commotion of teenagers coming and going at all hours and it's doubtful she got much sleep.

The rest of the summer was filled with other guests, all wanting to go St. Helen's. I'm getting to be quite the tour guide.

One day this fall, I was feeling a little nauseous so asked Robin to get me one of my Prevacid tablets. As I waited at the bathroom door, I watched her turn on the water, get the pill, and promptly swallow it. "Now can I have one?" I asked. It is a good thing it wasn't my Premerin. I'm not sure how it would have affected her.

May you have a wonderful holiday with the ones you love and be able to tolerate the ones you don't.

Love, Shirley, drug pusher

Niece Darlene and me

CHRISTMAS 1990

Hi from Old Blue's blues,

During our February snow/ice week, I had visitors from Wyoming. My niece, Darlene, and husband, Tod, came to the coast to check out a job Tod was interested in. They laughed at the closing of schools, but they changed their minds after witnessing a horrendous accident on the icy freeway during their journey to Salem, Oregon. Our country of many steep hills and tight curves are not as conducive to vehicle safety as the straight, flat terrain of Wyoming.

One morning in March, Old Blue just wouldn't start AGAIN. I had Robin bundle me up, told her to go on to her college classes (she has her own car), and I headed out to school. On the hill's sidewalk, I encountered a softball-sized rock. If I went on one side of it, I would end up in the ditch, the other side on the busy highway. My only choice was to straddle it. WRONG MOVE. The next thing I knew, I was face down in the ditch with my chair on top of me. A kindly state worker had seen me flip, stopped, uprighted the chair and deposited me into it. After inquiring if I was hurt, with me answering with 'nothing but my vanity', he went on his way before I could get his name to thank him for not leaving me there for the ditch varmints to gnaw on me. No time to go home and change clothes. Onward I went to work, covered from head to toe with mud. By the time I arrived, everyone who was already at school knew I had had an 'accident' as some student on his way to the middle school had seen my unfortunate incident, had reported it to Rose who works there, she had called the H.S. secretary who had sent the principal rushing to save his harebrained teacher once again. Dorothy, our secretary, managed to de-mud my face and hands, but the clothes had to remain in muddy disarray for the remainder of the day. It did provide a lesson in safety for my students.

At home, I decided I was not going to depend on Old Blue any longer, took a day off, and Robin and I paid a visit to the handicapped van store in Portland. There they informed me that a company in New Mexico had devised a way to lower a mini van, outfit it with an automatic door and ramp, remove the front seats, put in automatic lock-downs and add hand controls. Oh what independence I could have. Because these vans are modified to fit the owners' needs, I would have to wait 6-12 months to receive it. I ordered the van; but consequently, I had to depend on Old Blue until the new one arrived.

Some friends had purchased a hot tub. While visiting them one day, they convinced me that I should try it out. I borrowed some shorts, was heaved over the edge and immediately went under, my head that is. My torso just floats, but my head and arms don't. I'd get my head up only to have it go under again. The jets were rolling me around like a beach ball. Finally, after drinking several cups of chlorinated water, my friends decided hot tubs were not for me and rescued me from its jaws.

While shopping one day, I went to the restroom. When finished, I told Shirley I would wait for her outside. As I left, a gentleman was holding open a door that I thought was the outside door back into the store. Thanking him, oops, I found myself in the men's restroom. I then knew why he looked at me quizzically. Yelling loudly for Shirley without success and noticing the door said "pull" not push, I pondered as to how I was going to explain my presence there when the next fellow walked in. I came to the conclusion that I'd just say I had brought my grandson in and he'd run out shutting the door behind him. However, I never had to utilize that excuse as Shirley, not finding me in the store, retraced her steps. Hearing her calling out to me, I answered. I had a hard time convincing her I was not in there in hopes of seeing some male's genitalia which I hadn't viewed in years.

Well, the latter is not quite true. I forgot about the porno magazine that was delivered to me addressed to the former resident of my duplex.

With that shocking news, I shall wish you all "good" thoughts and happy holidays.

Love, Shirley, voyeur

CHRISTMAS 1991

Hello from Plomondon Road,

Another catastrophe in the garage during a big freeze. This time, a pipe broke in the WALL. It doesn't pay to have unheated garages that are not insulated. The plumber had just been gone one day when the pipe to the washing machine froze. I decided I had better invest in a portable heater, but our local hardware was out of them, and it was too dangerous to travel to a bigger town. Finding the hair dryer wouldn't budge the ice from the pipe, I promised my bachelor neighbor a dinner if he would thaw it out with his blow torch. Mission accomplished. That afternoon, the weather warmed, ice on roads melted, but I still bought a heater... just in case.

A friend stopped by one day for a visit. Our conversation turned to the subject of my new van, which had just arrived a few days earlier. She proceeded to tell me how lucky I was to live in a country where modern technology had all but alleviated my handicap. "Quads are nearly equivalent to the fully functional human being," she expressed. Oh yeah! After thinking to myself, "Let her trade places with me for a day and she'd quickly change her mind". Rather than lose a friend to win an argument, I changed the subject.

Now to the van. It arrived in February, a sleek, gray minivan which was half the size of the Blue Whale. It was equipped with controls to lower or raise the back portion 12 inches, open the door and lower a small ramp for easy entering or exiting. The hand controls would allow me to once again drive. I was quite leery of the driving portion of this new vehicle, but Chuck assured me that with him instructing me while riding shotgun, I would soon be in control of this 5000 pounds of plastic, glass and steel hurtling down the road at breakneck speeds. However, my new wheelchair barely fit through the door. After many tries at twisting and turning, I was able to maneuver into position under the wheel. I made a diagram of the contortions and sent it to Patrick Swayze. He thanked me and said he would incorporate the diagrammed moves into his next movie, "Dirty Dancing II."

I was doing fine until I had to turn left. Left turns require the use of triceps and those muscles no longer listen to my brain telling them to get to work. My thoughts mulled over every possible way I could get to school doing only right turns. After circling the block several times, I noticed the neighbor across the street, who is also a policeman, checking me out. He meandered over inquiring as to why I was going around the block so many times. When I explained the situation of only right turns, he told me if I managed to get to any destination using only right turns, he would have to give me a ticket for failure to do left turns. Funny cop. After several near misses and me being afraid of causing an accident where someone else might end up like me, I abandoned the notion of driving.

In March, when returning from a family funeral in Idaho, Lynn, my new weekend help, and I stopped for the night at a motel. I pushed the remote to open the door and allow me to exit the vehicle. Nothing happened. I looked again at the remote to make sure I was pushing the "open" button and still nothing moved. Not a click, whir or beep. With my frustration mounting, I had thoughts of violence toward the inventors of my gray prison. "Read the instruction manual, " a voice in my thoughts murmured. We enacted the emergency door and lift release and I was free... Lynn was not cheery about performing this ritual every time I wanted out. The next day, I was quarantined to the van for the ride home. Food and water were served to me through the front door, but I was not allowed out until we were back in Toledo. A trip to Portland to the dealer alleviated the problem.

Spring vacation. Because Robin's college doesn't have the same week for their break, I convinced Angela, another helper, and her friend, Kim, that it would be fun to head south to Las Vegas and my Arizona friends, the Breneman's. As we were driving across the 110°-heated desert, the Gray Shark (as the kids christened it) started leaping like a bucking bronco. We limped into a not-too-inviting rest stop where a trucker informed us we were experiencing vapor lock. "Let it sit for 20 minutes and it will be fine," he explained. To make sure, we waited 30. The shade from the one lone tree didn't keep us from near heat stroke, so we stayed in the restroom continually splashing water on each other. On the road again. We had gone just a few miles and the Shark attacked again. We turned around and leaped back to the rest stop. I called IMS from whom I had purchased the van. They were as perplexed as we were. No help there. Back to the restroom where we stayed until dark. The cooler air allowed us to get to a motel down the highway toward Vegas.

Visualize this:

Up, dressed and having eaten breakfast, we venture off once more. The Shark is being good when at about noon we enter Vegas. I guess he doesn't like the looks of this place for in the middle of the busiest intersection, he again begins to gyrate, backfire, leap and then die, enveloping Kim into the folding chair she has been sitting in. Horns honk, people yell and give us finger gestures, Kim and Angie are laughing hysterically, I'm mortified and wondering how we are going to extricate Kim who looks like a frog in a hamburger press. Angie gets the Shark started once more. With the van still leaping, we manage to get to the service station on the corner. No help there. We decide to abandon the Shark in their parking area, drag out the luggage and tromp to a 19th century motel in that block. Luckily they have a room for us. I then call MGM and cancel our reservation. We meander down the Strip, I lose $20 to the mafia, and we take in a couple of free shows. We are exhausted and go back to the motel around midnight. We are sleeping soundly when all of a sudden, we get banging, screeching, laughter and doors slamming from the room directly above us. I call the front desk. That is no help as what do we expect, this is Vegas where no one but us wants to sleep. Against my protests, Ang goes up to try and convince them to quiet down. She comes back disgusted. They are Orientals, all drunk and not a one of them speaks English. They finally leave at seven and so do we. The Shark appears to be cured. We manage to get to our destination without the Shark throwing another tantrum. After two days of Breneman hospitality, we head for L.A. and home. At Indio, he throws another fit. We pull into a store there. Ang goes in to ask if they know of a garage nearby that we might manage to leap to. All speak Spanish and don't understand what she wants. We buy some fruit, cheese, crackers, drinks (no, not alcoholic, but I think that might have helped) and enjoy our lunch in the shade of the store's trees. We then buy some paperbacks and read until evening. We have decided the Shark is a vampire.

We find a garage open on the outskirts of L.A. Again they diagnose vapor lock. We see a motel sign a couple of blocks away with a vacancy. I am tired, lie down for a nap in my bra and unders as I am overheated, while the girls go for a stroll. Just as I am nodding off, in walks a man. "Gotta mud these walls. Painters coming tomorrow," he says while I am trying to explain my near nudity and why I'm not able to cover up. Girls come back with dinner; hamburgers and fries. Then yelling next door. She's screaming about her purse. He takes his truck and leaves. She's still yelling about that purse. We go to bed, but we don't get much sleep as a family right out of "The Grapes of Wrath" on the other side of us spend the night working on their old dilapidated truck. We finally give up, get up at four and head up the coast route where it is cooler. The Gray Shark is happy and behaving. After a peaceful night of sleep in Eureka, CA, we finally arrive home. Can you believe that Robin is jealous of our "fun"?

A few phone calls at home reveal the pitfalls of technology. Everyone can diagnose the problem, but no one will take the responsibility to fix it. IMS says it is endemic to all minivans of that year and model. The manufacturer says it is the conversions that cause the problems. Finally, a local garage tells me they think the fuel pump is too small to take care of the extra weight the conversion carries. A bigger pump is installed, and I hope that the next time I journey out of the temperate Pacific Northwest, I can travel during the day with no leaps and bounds instead of like a ghost rider in the night.

In June, I moved to a larger house in the country. It is still about the same distance to the school with no BIG hill.

Robin had to leave for a job she can handle while going to nursing school. I hired Charity, a sweet girl I know from school. She had just been with me for one day when I got quite sick. Three days of that and I got no better. I went to emergency to find that I not only had kidney infection but also pneumonia. A few days later, after the doctor had told me that I would someday probably die from either one or the other of those ailments, and clutching a gigantic hospital bill, I was able to go home.

Charity and I were sleeping soundly when I heard an awful crash. Thinking that a tree had hit the house, I yelled for Charity, but she was already investigating. A drunk had missed the corner at the end of our driveway and had landed in our yard, taking out a small tree and several rhododendrons. He had no insurance and no driver's license. He did give me his name. I found out later that his license was suspended because of a former DUI. In case it happened again, I had my neighbor, who has a construction company, bring me a large boulder that he placed at the spot. No driver had better miss that corner again or it will be him that is damaged.

Back at work, the weather was beautiful and I decided to wheel home. I had just left the school grounds when a belt broke on my chair. With no control, I wheeled right into a patch of blackberry bushes. There I sat, waving both arms; drivers waved back. "Do they think I am here picking blackberries in October?" I asked myself. I couldn't believe when I noticed one of them was Wendy, my former fainting aide. Even a neighbor went by and waved, but I noticed him turn around and come back. Bless Dick! Not capable of lifting my heavy chair by himself, he went to the school and got coach Bruce to help. With me plunked onto the front seat and the chair in the back of his pickup, they took me home. There they sat me in front of the TV, stashed the control and my cordless phone in my lap and left. "Call if you need help," Dick ordered. Twenty minutes later the power went off. There I was, a blank TV, cordless phone needing electricity for use and me wondering how long it would be until Dick realized I couldn't call. Two hours later, Teddy came by, pushed me to the kitchen table, gave me a book to read and HE left. The sun went down, and the power came on, but I couldn't move to reach the light switch nor the telephone that had been left in the living room. Four very long, dark hours later Charity came home from the conference she had been attending. Aw, release from boredom.

Robin's dad lives down the road and since he is the shop teacher, I thought he might have a belt that would work for the wheel. He didn't, but found one at a car parts store. The next day, I ordered a new chair.

Modern technology? On those days when my wheelchair dies and I'm left facing a blank wall watching the paint, or I swelter in the van on a hot day because the computer-controlled door won't open, or I lie in a ditch where my errant w/c dumped me, I reflect on my friend's comment about how lucky I am to have these modern conveniences. A jingle from a commercial sings in my mind, "At GE, we bring good things to life!"

November brought heavy rains. House problems again. The drain field line backed up. The basement flooded. The water came in faster than the sump pump could suck it out. The landlord refused to do anything, explaining that he had tried everything he knew to fix the problem that apparently occurs every rainy season. I searched the yellow pages where I found a company that guaranteed they could fix any leaking basement. After putting three trenches in the basement floor, installing drainpipes, recementing, digging holes along the outside walls every two feet and pouring in some kind of adhesive, I was left, hopefully, with a non-leaking basement, but with a $1500 bill which the landlord refused to pay and a very toxic smell every time it rained.

Has your brain gone numb by now? It should have, mine has. So au revoir for this year.

MERRY CHRISTMAS... Love to all, Shirley

The Goodalls moved in!
Ross Stinger, Tod, Darlene, Tanya, Hattie Stinger, Tyeanna, Tessa, Joshua, and me

CHRISTMAS 1992

Hello From Looneyville,

My new chair arrived in February. A sleek aluminum alloy frame undercarriage with quick-release-driven hubs and a micro-controlled joystick was a triumph of technology and a welcome replacement to my conventional chair with its belts and flimsy frame. It was a computerized haven. However, behind all of that lay a disaster.

It came without the handles that protrude from the back of a conventional chair. I use these to help position myself and to hold on when in motion. Without them, I flopped around like a freshly caught fish on the riverbank. The dealer installed handles, but they had sharp edges that cut my underarms and lacerated my clothing. Jim, the high school metal shop teacher, and some of his students removed these, bent some smooth water pipe and bolted them on for handles. The blood-letting stopped.

Those high tech quick-release hubs added four inches to the width of the chair causing me to leave my 'mark' on the door frames, doors and walls at home as well as at the school. When calling the manufacturer (a Canadian company) their solution was: remodel the house. They've got to be kidding! The reclining seat back gave way one day, leaving me with my feet dangling off the front and my head dangling off the rear. Painted gold, I could have passed as one of McDonald's arches. Disgusted, I prevailed on Chuck to write a letter to the company, listing what was wrong with the chair and giving suggestions on how to correct the problems. He never got an answer.

During the first two months of ownership, I had to return to my old chair eight times while the front wheel bearings were replaced, the motors were repaired after shorting out and the computer brain was being operated on. Plus one evening while my Tharp friends came to visit, my chair started accelerating on its own to speeds equal to those of the Indy 500. Blaming Erin for this sudden movement, which she continually denied, Jim released the power cord, stopping the chair. During the next few days, it did it again, and again and again.

I gave up on the chair, and took it back to the dealer, but they didn't want it nor would they refund my money as "you have modified it." I ordered another chair from my old, reliable company. In the meantime, I reverted back to using the old belted one, which appeared to have lost at a demolition derby.

In April, my brother Bill passed away. This was the brother who had carried me everywhere as a child as he was so grateful that my parents had produced a girl instead of one of the male gender like the previous eight had been. I had also lived with him and his wife, Mary, during the "dark years" post accident. I shall miss this quiet, gentle man.

I woke up one night to a noise that sounded like a piece of wood moving across the basement floor. I recalled we had left a basement window open so assumed a possum had decided to take up residence there. About the time of the third such noise, Charity awoke, and came running in to get in bed with me. She was sure it was a rapist coming to do us in. She then called her deputy-sheriff dad who came with his gun drawn to investigate. He could find nothing amiss, shut the window and made sure all doors were locked. After several nights of those nocturnal noises, we deduced it was the cat, not the Cat Burglar, on the roof and not in the basement as we had formerly thought. Too bad it isn't the "Hot Tin Roof" as we can't keep her down.

Speaking of basement, the drainpipes and sealing have kept us from having to burn up the motor on another shop vac. Not one drop of water on the basement floor, but I'm not visualizing installing carpet again as yet.

School was out in early June for the students but not for me. I had to take summer classes in Seattle. A two-hour journey once per week. On one of these occasions, since my new replacement chair still had not arrived and I was having to rely on the old one, I found myself stranded in the middle of an intersection. Again with the honking horns, yelling, and gestures. Charity got my beast in neutral and with huffing and puffing, as it is as heavy as a John Deere tractor, she managed to get me out of the way before we were arrested for impeding traffic. I don't know which one worked, her banging or my cursing, but I managed to be in control once more.

Back to Seattle the next week, with Lynn as chauffeur, to catch a ferry for a class on location. As we were getting a ferry schedule, two men who had been arguing near us began fighting aggressively. The bigger fellow was pummeling and driving the other's head into the cement. Blood was flying, but everyone but us went about moving on or turning their backs. Being from a small town, we were not used to seeing this ungentlemanly behavior. Lynn spied a policeman down the street and reported it. He, too, seemed unconcerned. We felt we had done our duty, caught the ferry, absorbed some knowledge and retuned to the van only to find what we assumed was either a drunken or drugged-out homeless man hiding under newspapers and flopped directly in front of my ramp door. "Please move," I pleaded in my most ladylike voice. No response, not even a quiver. I repeated with more authority. Still not a budge. Lynn refused to get near enough to nudge him. "Move or you'll be squished like a bug beneath my chair wheels." He moved a couple of inches. "Lower the ramp on him," I commanded, which she did. He moved away, but you guessed it, right behind us where we would have to back up over him. Not wanting to get blood on my nice Michelin tires, I was at a loss as to what to do next. Just then another scraggly-looking soul came by, saw the situation, gave the poor hunk of humanity a hard football kick, which did the trick, and without a word moved on with us shouting "thank you, thank you" until he was out of sight.

Tod, Darlene, four kids and two dogs moved in during July. Tod got a job as an electrician at Weyerhaeuser, but they will stay with me until they get a house built. Tod and Darlene sleep in their camp trailer, kids on the den floor. My brother, Ross, and his wife, Hattie, who are Darlene's parents, came to help erect the new residence. While waiting to get land bought, Tod and my brothers, Ross, Keith and Addy remodeled my garage adding a second bath, insulation (no freezing pipes ever again), sheet rock and a new, wider, power door needed since Katie, when working for me, had denuded my van of both side mirrors. While Darlene was off making land deals, Hattie, with her usual mothering skills, kept us fed and the house in pristine order.

Charity left for a Missouri college in August and Darlene became my hands and legs until I could find new help.

At home alone while everyone was working on the Goodall's house, I went into my office to get a pen; in the middle of the floor, I blew another fuse. %&* A wall and a door can get very boring if you have to stare at them for any extended time. A student came to borrow my school keys and pushed me, with pen in hand, back to the dining room table where I could work on my crossword puzzle.

For the next two weeks, the kids and I went to Chuck and Sally's each day to feed their cat and dog while they were on vacation. On one of these jaunts, a bearing on my w/c went out. I crept home and am now relegated to my push chair.

Late August, I found new help, Harmony. School started, house full of people, confusion, confusion, but somehow Hattie kept us all in sync. In November, Ross had finished all that he could help with on the house, and he and Hattie departed for their Utah home. The Goodalls hope to be in their own house by the first of the year.

The newly ordered chair has not yet arrived. I donated the 'other' new one to a lady in Vader who just needs it when she has to leave her house, which isn't often.

Even with these many malfunctions, I can only laugh. Hopefully, I'll make it through the holidays with no van, chair or basement problems.

So it goes.   Love, Shirley

Basking in some rare Washington sunshine at Mayfield Lake. Family Reunion

CHRISTMAS 1993

Hi from Duckville,

Duckville? This country is certainly suited for those fine-feathered, web-footed creatures but not for this unfeathered, non-web-footed piece of humanity.

This year brought its usual dilemmas: some shared with the neighbors and some I retained for me alone. A cold front fell upon our area in January, bringing with it winds that reached up to 80 mph and taking the power lines with it. While my students and I watched trees bending to and fro or being uprooted completely, the administration was wondering how they were going to get the kiddies home with most roads blocked with fallen firs. (With the power off, school cannot be in session.) After several hours with the school feeling as if Jack Frost stepped in with all of his relatives, causing students to bundle up like Eskimos, we were informed that the buses could get through as our Ever-readies (no not the batteries but our local loggers) had been out in force with power saws cutting paths through our fallen virgins (timber, that is). I reached home to find Darlene sopping up the basement. Even though it had been good about keeping dry, it needed the sump pump to perform that duty. No electricity, no sump pumps. The fire department came to our rescue, but it was like the tide going in and out. After several calls, Darlene found a small generator to rent, not knowing that she was going to be up all night refueling it every two hours, and regenerating the generator each time it broke down, which was often. Each time we went to heat something in the microwave, turned on a light or got a drink, it refused to spout forth the power to perform these duties.

We were truly roughing it here in the wilds. By morning they had the power back on at the school and other public facilities, enabling me to return to civilization (stinking, greasy haired, smelly breathed) only to find that most of my contemporaries had spent the night in motels in Castle Rock, Kelso and Longview as the North Wind bloweth not in those areas. On the third day, Darlene borrowed a camp stove, went to Longview to get some kerosene for lamps (all sold out locally) and came home to power. Because she had listed me with the PUD as an "invalid" (ha) we got priority status. For the next three days, we were the source for friends to shower, get water and some even came for dinner; they brought the fixings, we provided the power. Then a warming up and floods. On this hill, we were spared the swimming!

Van illnesses abounded. The power steering got a deadly groaning disease. I had to rent another handicapped van at, ugh, $250/day while the operation took place. It was a quick surgery of one day. Then on a routine service call, the power steering sprung a leak, dripped onto the hot motor inflicting third degree burns. This time it was hospitalized for six days while I braved the roads again via wheelchair. During the next three weeks, the main depressor depressed. They just got that healed when I had to call the auto ambulance again for another problem with the power steering. The van surgeon asked me if I would like to put him on permanent salary. I told him I thought I had.

In August, Hattie, Charity and I took some of my nieces and nephews to Mt. Rainier for a scenic tour. On the way home, Hattie started complaining about the bruises that were being inflicted on her posterior as she rode along in the back of the Shark. We deduced that a major spring was practicing its floor exercises for the Olympics only to find the next day that the compressor that raises and lowers the van had died. A call to IMS, an overnight delivery and a quick transplant by Tod alleviated the dragging, or so we thought. Hissing snakes??? No. 'Twas a hole in the air bag caused from dragging our rear home from the mountain. Another IMS call and overnight delivery.

Unfortunately, what was guaranteed to be a thirty-minute installation took both Tod and Son four hours. One week later, the relay on the compressor decided to quit relaying its messages, necessitating a repeat IMS call. However, this was a simple surgery of two minutes performed by Charity (Harmony left, Charity returned). Later in October, Charity, on a routine errand for an oil change, got one mile out of town, and the van decided it was not ready for its oil transfusion and refused to go any further. Another call for the auto ambulance. "Heart problems," the auto doctor explained. We waited another five days for the alternator to be replaced. Luckily, November sneaked in and out with no further office calls.

At the end of basketball season, my principal's wife, Bonnie, offered to chauffeur me to a nearby town to watch the boys play in the play-offs. While Bonnie chatted with some friends post game, I decided I would go ahead to the van, lower the ramp and wheel in. So going at my usual souped-up speed, I headed out the door onto a poorly lit walkway, missed the cut out ramp, jumped a 1-1/2 inch curb and landed on my face in front of four men who wondered what apparition was groveling at their feet. Again, nothing was hurt but my vanity. Have you ever seen four men trying to put a giant rubber band (me) in a chair? Bonnie did. She said it was a sight she would never forget.

The new chair arrived at the dealer's in Portland. Now, being fitted for a new chair is like being fitted for dentures. By darn, I'm going to be living with it, hopefully, for a long time, and it had better be comfy. After eight trips to Portland or them to me, it now fits like an old pair of shoes. It is back-heavy because of two 12-volt batteries. Wheelie bars were installed to prevent backward flips. These, though, had to be removed as they caught on the school thresholds. Whoopee. As I entered the van, I did a 90-degree flip, cracked the old skull open AGAIN, plus this time, pulling some shoulder muscles. Now the bars are back on, straightened somewhat allowing for door escapage.

The Goodalls moved into their "garage home" in April leaving this a very quiet house once again, too quiet.

They say things happen in threes. But can't I be spared this adage just once? My heat pump went out the same week as my razor and make-up mirror. The former, the landlord took care of, but he didn't seem to care about the latter two. He secretly thought (I assumed) he could use the bristly legs for brushes for his cattle (that graze next door), and my face to scare away the rustlers!!

Out of stories, out of time.

A joyous season to all,

Shirley

CHRISTMAS 1994

A message from Toledo,

Because the first six months of the year were spent with the usual breakdowns of my van's special equipment, I determined it was time to quit dealing with the "jerk" in Portland and go to the installers; therefore, in June I made arrangements to take the Shark to IMS in Farmington, New Mexico. To help Charity with the driving, I convinced my friend, Bobbi, that she would have a lifetime experience by joining us. It turned out to be a typical Watson escapade!

Two hours from home, my nephew, Calvin, was our first stop. Upon leaving, we said our goodbyes, reentered the van and prepared to depart. The van was not cooperating. It refused to start. However the Shark was not to blame. Charity had left the lights on. Minor problem. Jump-start and we were off. Stopped for a picnic lunch. Ramp door wouldn't open. Used emergency escape mechanism. Rear window wiper refused to wipe off the downpour of rain, but to our amazement, it fixed itself after a couple of hours. Already Bobbi was beginning to wonder what I had gotten her into. As we drove over Grants Pass, the van heated up. "No way, " I exclaimed, "not in 65-degree rainy weather." We located a Dodge dealership. They installed a new thermostat, air filter and flushed out the cooling system while we had dinner at a Chinese restaurant across the street. Hoping to make some points with the manager, we took him the leftover Chinese (food, that is) but our bill didn't reflect our generosity. We drove to Redding, CA, got a motel, and collapsed.

We had called ahead to make reservations at a motel near my nephew, Steven's, but when we arrived at the motel, they had never heard of us, and all rooms were full because of visitor's day at the military base nearby. Steven's direction to his house didn't work either as they had renamed one of the streets without him knowing. While we were searching for the nonexistent street, Bobbi missed the 10 mph warning sign, hit some 'undulations' at 30 mph, and Charity, who had released her seat belt minutes before to ask at a station for better direction and had not rebelted, shot into the air like a released champagne cork, hit the ceiling, and plummeted onto the cooler, while luggage attacked her from the back. She was scraped and bruised, which required having first aid by Physician Assistant, Steven. Our visit was cut short, as we had to travel on to find other accommodations.

As we traversed across the Mohave Desert, the Shark once again screamed, "I'm hot!" I then remembered the trick of turning the heater on to remove heat from the engine. "You've got to be kidding. It's 120° out," screamed driver, Bobbi. It worked, but all three felt like we were being roasted alive. Half an hour later we arrived at the city of Lost Wages, as Bobbi dubbed it, and planted our overheated bodies at the MGM Grand. I was watching Bobbi playing blackjack when some young, inebriated Irishmen insisted I was bringing them good luck and wouldn't let me leave. I might have fallen for his winsome ways, but I decided he was too young, and determined it was better to spread my charm elsewhere. A stroll up the strip found us battling winds so hard that I had difficulty keeping my chair on the sidewalk as we "strolled" the mile to capture the eruption of the volcano at the Mirage. We arrived at 12:08 a.m. It had ceased to cooperate. It doesn't belch after 12:00. Oh well, it wouldn't have held a candle to our "Heaving Helen" at home. The return trip was no better. We arrived back at the MGM, me in tears (dust under my contacts), only to find that Sticky Fingers Louie or one of his henchmen had lifted my billfold from beside me in the chair. I only lost $30, but my insurance and credit cards plus I.D. might have been needed before this trip ended. I was so mad I sent myself to bed without supper.

After calls to my credit card companies, we were on the road again. When we stopped for gas and lunch, the ramp wouldn't deploy. Back to the manual emergency backup system. A breakdown on the way to Dr. Mechanic? Unheard of!

IMS were great hosts. They picked us up at the motel, and while work was being done on my van, they took us through the plant where they do 75 conversions each month. You would have thought I was a foreign dignitary. The owner, Greg Ansel, had to meet me to thank me for "keeping him in business" for four years; also the parts and shipping clerks had to view this person who had kept them occupied shipping replacements. Greg (who also owns the Burger King chain) explained that since mine--- one of their first--- was built, they had made many improvements. This we witnessed in the plant only to make me desirous for one of the new super models. After replacing parts (plus supplying some for future use), I asked for the dreaded bill. "No charge," I was told. A worthwhile trip, as have had no "special" problems since. The rest have been Dodge snags.

The next day we took a side trip to Durango, Colorado, to take a ride on the train from which Butch Cassidy once helped himself to some cash, only to miss the last trip by 10 minutes. Backtracked toward Flagstaff. Stopped for Bobbi to take a picture.

"What's this? A cloud of smoke coming from the engine?" We pulled into a desert oasis equipped with one gas pump, an outhouse, and a grizzled-looking fellow of 80+ who knew as much about cars as I knew about space stations. Two fellows in an 18-wheeler tried to help, but unfortunately, they spoke an undetermined language. We finally, through gestures, understood it would be all right to go the 20 miles to Flagstaff. We canceled our reservations in Phoenix, and spent our evening hunting for accommodations in a town that was having its annual rodeo celebration. We passed up the 8' by 8' Xmas cabins for a $120 room at Holiday Inn. We found a garage owned by a nice young couple open on Sunday that fixed the transmission fluid leak well enough to get us home.

In Phoenix, of the 3 people I was going to visit, none were available. We decided to go to Yuma only to find the A/C didn't work, and it was 117° out at 6 pm. Another day was wasted getting that fixed. On to Yuma, crossed the border to Alagondas, Mexico at 7 pm. All of the shops were closed so Charity never got her authentic Mexican dinner. I got up the next morning, plopped into my chair, and headed for the bathroom. The chair was being self-willed. It refused to move. We had planned to cross the border again but couldn't find a w/c repairman in Yuma who worked on motorized chairs so had to forgo Mexico once again and headed for San Diego to the dealer my Portland salesman recommended via telephone. We had to employ our heater method again over the Sierras. By the time we reached a lower elevation again, Charity groaned that we could bury her then and there as she was already cremated.

We got the chair temporarily fixed the next day, but was told I would have to have a new control panel... still under warranty... when I got home. Our stay in San Diego consisted of looking for a friend who had moved (no luck), going to Old Town, Hotel Del Coronado, and Tijuana, the latter I never care to visit again. However, I love S.D, as their year-round moderate climate is perfect for me.

On our way to Disneyland, we stopped at the Wild Animal Park, which I usually enjoy, but it was too hot for this trip. We took Bobbi to her grandfather's in Pasadena where she stayed the night. On our way back to Anaheim, Charity and I got lost in downtown L.A. We saw a policeman, asked directions, he stopped 6 lanes so we could make a U-turn to get on the correct street, and off we went. Two miles later we had not found the bridge where we were supposed to turn and found ourselves in the Watts district. Finally we saw someone we thought was a policeman. Charity rolled down the window and said "Sir" about three times. He finally pointed down the street and said, "Go 2 blocks and turn left." How he knew we wanted I-5 still puzzles me. At Disneyland the next day, the "airbag" that raises the van, developed a crater. IMS gave us the # to call in North

Hollywood, 40 miles hence. "Yes, we can fix it tomorrow," Mr. Fixit said. We enjoyed Disneyland; around midnight Bobbi's aunt came to steal her away, and Charity and I went back to the motel. The next day we bumped our way... I-5 in L.A. resembles the Craters of the Moon... to replace the old bag (the van's, not me). Bobbi, her aunt, and cousin met us across the street for lunch. Bobbi and Charity almost suffered cardiac arrest because Bob Hope was having lunch two tables from us. The star-struck duo got no autographs, not allowed at this restaurant.

From Hollywood to home was uneventful as far as "disasters" go. Upon arrival in Toledo, I sighed, and decided I was not meant for travel..... but in two or three years, who knows! Since then, I did get the transmission fixed, the w/c restored to full power and new brakes installed.

The rest of my summer was spent relaxing with houseguests, some short trips to see friends, and then back to work.

This has not been a good year so far. I have some students with some difficult problems, the worst of which is their off-the-wall behavior. Should I end the school year with all my hair and faculties in tact, it will be a miracle. Without my faithful teacher assistant, Sherri, I would probably have left some tread marks on some faces by now. She is better than I at keeping her "cool."

The loss of my sister-in-law, Naomi, this fall was difficult for she was a part of my family before I was born.

May this holiday find you with some events to look forward to in the New Year. Mine is to find some paralyzing blow darts to use on a few KIDS!!

Love, Shirley, the harried traveler/teacher

No wheelchair ramps during Captain Cook's time...

CHRISTMAS 1995

Winter passed with no major breakdowns from the van, the chair or me.

The school purchased me a new computer. I had learned enough on the old one to write a basic letter or report, but this one is the latest in technical brainpower. It has so many options that if I could grasp even one aspect of it a day, I'd still be learning far into the next century. I'll learn the basics and leave the in-depth workings to the more astute. Thinking I had those basics down pat, I had written a lengthy report when I was rewarded with it landing somewhere in Siberia. I have now learned to save my work every few paragraphs.

I had read about a replica of the old sailing vessel that Captain Cook had explored the Northwest with, and decided it would be fun to take the outing through Puget Sound that they offered. Being assured I could get aboard with my chair, my friend, Fran, Charity and I headed to Seattle for a day's outing. Tickets purchased, we waited our turn, but where was the ramp? "Ramp? We have a method more fitting for an old ship." PICTURE THIS. A crowd on the waterfront pointing at a slightly embarrassed old lady being jerry rigged to a block and tackle preparing for a heist up and over the side. Going up wasn't too frightening, but when deploying, the ship was listing --- list leeward and I'd swing out, list to the starboard and I'd swing in. However, the rigging masters got it steadied and I was once again on terra firma.

Just this week, the switch went out on my chair the second time since August. I got a sub, took the day off, and Katie and I plowed through the inch-deep rain to the repair shop in Portland. Within 30 minutes, I was mobile again, and since I had a replacement on the job, we decided to do some Christmas shopping. We had gone into a shop where I had exited before Katie. While sitting there people-watching, I felt a tap on my shoulder. Thinking it was Katie, I made some trendy remark, but was shocked when I looked up. There stood the mall security guard. "M'am," he muttered. "Would you please slow down while in the mall?" After explaining to him that I had been in the chair for some years and was an experienced driver, he said, "But we have a lot of shoppers at this time of the year and those people don't know that so I've had complaints." For some reason, it has slipped my mind to mention it to Katie. Would you have told her if you had spent the last 2-1/2 years trying to convince her, while driving my van, she wasn't Mario Andretti?

This week has been a usual Watson headache. The motor in the sump pump failed, my lock-down for my chair in the van broke, and the monitor for this computer developed a loose connection to its brain. Are you a high tech troubleshooter and repairman and wish to live in the fashion of Bill Gates? Come to Toledo. I'll keep you in business.

Have a great year.

Love, Shirley

CHRISTMAS 1996

When I moved from town to the country, I was not sure I had made the right decision. The construction company next door wakes me at 5:00 each morning as they head out with their trucks and machinery for a day's labor, the cattle rancher is constantly separating a calf from its mother resulting in enough noise to put an angry bunch of football fans to shame and the wind blows harder and more often than it did in the valley below where I previously resided. However, I decided after this past winter that living on a hill had its compensations. My house became the refuge for my homeless friends when our area was hit with not only one flood but later another.

Since the flooding basement problem has been rectified, I have been relieved of my private basement swimming pool. In March while I was "educating students," Mr. North Wind decided that my state of affairs had been too serene and set about correcting the situation. He sent trees across the power lines; good-bye the current to my sump pump. School shut down and we were sent home. Alas, I found my basement flooded once more. We got the generator started and called the fire department. They were out on an actual "fire" call, but bless those men, as soon as they could, they once again pumped out the offending water. I then put in a claim to my rental insurance only to be told that I couldn't claim something that was caused by an act of God. Had I known that, my hot water tank would mysteriously have sprung a leak; that would have been covered. I enlisted several of my students to drag the soggy carpet out and convey it to the dump. No sweat, we'll just survive with cement floors. A short time later, Rose and

In Hawaii once again, with Charity

Son decided to replace their carpet, offered me their old but still serviceable one, and laid it down for me. No more cold tootsies while doing laundry. Hopefully, this is the last carpet caper.

It was time for my six-month dental appointment. As we headed out, I decided I could have traveled as fast by w/c as the Shark would not shift from low gear. It took us 25 minutes to go seven miles. I rescheduled the dental appointment. A tow was made to the dealer where a new tranny was installed. I was back to wheeling to school. However, this time I was blessed with nice April sunshine. BUT it seems that with every blessing, I get a demon on my shoulder. As I was wheeling along enjoying the warm rays, I sensed disaster. Those clouds moving in fast looked quite ominous. All of a sudden, I was being pelted with hailstones. Ah, I spied the Rico's carport empty. Shelter at last. Ten minutes later, the offenders had moved on, and although wet, I was not pitted!

A friend took Katie to retrieve the van. I swear that girl needs glasses or a lesson in depth perception. Another rear view mirror lost its life as she pulled into the garage.

As I was soundly asleep, I was awakened by hearing a big crash. Assuming a picture had fallen off the wall, I decided not to wake up the living dead. Morning arrived; dressed, I headed for the kitchen. There in the middle of the floor lay the large fluorescent ceiling fixture along with plaster and sheet rock. Had anyone been standing in that spot, they would have suffered Excedrin headache #98.

In July, my niece from Boise moved in to be my caregiver. She brought with her two of her grandchildren, Alyx, four, and Amanda, five. This has certainly changed my style of living. No more quiet evenings. Those two kids fight like banty chickens. What mischief one of them doesn't think to get into, the other one does. One can only hope that will change as time marches on.

I went to my rescheduled dentist appt. This reminded me of a former dental appointment that I was headed for when I had my accident. I was told while under the anesthesia to have holes drilled into my skull to attach the Crutchfield tongs he was installing, that I kept insisting that the surgeon was "drilling in the wrong place." In my unconscious state, I apparently thought I was in the dentist's chair.

In July, my friend, Phyllis, mother of Robin, my once-upon-a-time Girl Friday, informed me that if I could get the cash for a ticket, we could go to Honolulu where she has a condo. Both Charity and I combined resources and to Hawaii we headed. I know, I know. I said I'd never venture over the ocean again after my previous horrendous trip. At least this time, I was with pals. We flew Northwest. Those flight attendants couldn't do enough for me. We had bulkhead seats providing lots of legroom, pillows for dangling feet and warm air. This trip, though, was not without its mishaps. We had arranged for Flying Wheels to meet us at the airport and transport us to the condo. Done. Since it was late, and having had dinner on the plane, we immediately went to bed. Morning came, we dressed, had continental breakfast and headed out for sightseeing. As I was boarding the elevator, the door came shut on my w/c switch, breaking it. I could still move, but it had to be fixed, as there was no way to shut it off. The consequence, a dead battery. Phyllis called Flying Wheels; I rented a modified minivan similar to mine. Off to a w/c shop we headed, we thought. Alas, before we got out of the parking lot, the man who delivered the van slammed the door shut onto my w/c control, blowing out my computerized module. At the w/c shop, I was told they did not stock modules anywhere on the islands. So what else is new? I swallowed my need for independence, rented a pushchair and on we went to explore Hawaii. Despite the inconvenience, we had a great time. We still chuckle about the beach bums (they WERE cute) who tried desperately to hook up with Charity. We had been warned that their intentions were to secure free food and lodging.

Fall and back at school. I was pleasantly surprised to find that the two boys who had made my life miserable the previous year had decided not to return.

May you all be blessed with health and wealth in this coming year.

Shirley

CHRISTMAS 1997

In January, I had had to take a few days off from school because of a bad cold. I can see you smirking over taking leave for a cold, but as you know, I am unique. I have no active muscles in my chest, so someone has to push on my diaphragm for me to cough up what seemed like a bushel of junk. After several nights without sleep, Son and Rose came to visit. In his hand, Son had a large mug. "Drink this down and don't take time to breathe," he ordered. I managed most of it, when the fire started, my stomach crept up to my throat and flames were shooting from between my teeth. I had to take a breath. Whatever it was, it didn't stop my cold, but I certainly slept well that night.

That medicine reminded me of the sagebrush tea my dad brewed up for us when we were ill. He thought it cured everything from colds to appendicitis. He was probably right, as we would just as soon die before admitting we were sick, as we did not want to drink Dad's "bitter than gall" medicine.

On my desk at school, I have a very small space heater as I am always cold in the areas that I can feel—shoulders, neck, and head. As I was doing some paper work while my students were silently reading, I reached for a folder and caught my hand brace in the mesh of the heater front. My arm was jerking like an excited frog, an indication I was in pain. I yelled for a student to unplug the avenging arsonist, requested he go get the first aid teacher, while another student tried to release me from the clutches of the heater. That was accomplished just as the teacher/medic arrived. By then, my finger was so swollen that my ring was cutting off my circulation requiring another adult to get involved.

The shop teacher arrived with a small file; however, I was sure my finger was going to depart from my hand before they were able to saw through the ring. At last, blood once again flowed leaving me with a lovely blister about 1/2 in. high. Treated, bandaged and brace returned, I went on with the lesson; this one being on stupid things some people do to get male attention.

A few days later, I had taken off my brace and had it lying in my lap. I could only stand it on for short periods as it rubbed on my damaged finger. I was helping a student when the dern thing "jumped" from my lap onto the floor. As I turned my chair to see where it landed, I heard an ominous crunching sound. "OH, NO!" Another stupid maneuver. I enlisted two strong lads to tip my chair and retrieve my mangled best friend, my brace. Without it, I cannot perform my teaching duties. After school, I wheeled to the metal shop to see if the teacher could weld the broken halves back together.

"I'm sorry," he said. "I can't weld aluminum. It needs an arc welder which we don't have," he explained.

"Who would have one?" I asked.

He conferred with my principal and they agreed they might have one in the Trades Department of Lower Columbia College. Denny called. "Bring it in and we'll see what we can do," the teacher said. I took the next day off, went the 30 miles to LCC and within two hours it was fixed as good as new. No charge. Bless shop teachers everywhere. They have kept my chair and van running; made special devices I can use at work as well as at home, and are the most caring and generous people I know.

Alyx and Amanda like to stand on the battery case on my chair, and I take them for rides. One sunny day, I took Amanda and journeyed down the hill to our convenience store, bought each of us an ice cream, and trekked back toward home. As we neared a half-way point, we encountered a rather dilapidated car with an equally dilapidated, bearded man standing near it. He said, "Hi," and we returned his greeting. However we hadn't gone far when

I noticed the same car creeping along behind us. I envisioned this guy grabbing Amanda and taking off with her, and what could this old w/c woman do to stop him? Nothing! I became even more scared when we turned down our road, and he did likewise. Knowing no one was at home and noticing two neighbor men conversing down the road, I headed for them. The car picked up speed and took off. After explaining to Don why I interrupted his visit with his dad, I felt safe to go home. A few weeks later, during our town's annual festival, I encountered that same man. "You don't remember me, do you, Mrs. Watson?" he remarked. After saying his name, I did know him from school. But as all kids do, they change beyond recognition. "Why were you following us that day?" I inquired. "Well, I just wanted to make sure you and that little girl got home safe." he replied. Okay, so I'm overly cautious.

And that, my dears, are my trials of this year. Happy New Year.

Love,

Shirley, guardian of wee ones and sometimes taxi driver

CHRISTMAS 1998

With the Gray Shark still acting like a spoiled child, throwing tantrums and refusing to mind me, I decided to sell her, get as much moola from her potential buyer as I could, and use that as a down payment on a new more reliable vehicle. However I was hoodwinked by a fraudulent buyer, and eventually lost my court case along with a sack full of money. Could the loss have been due to the fact that this buyer's sister was the judge's secretary? I was bailed out of that forfeiture of funds by Linda and Jeremy Jaech (Linda is the daughter of my Breneman friends) who gave me enough stock that when sold amounted to more than the price of a new vehicle. Off to Snoqualmie to the van dealer. I asked my mechanical friend, Fran, to be my expert and accompany me. We came away with a nifty, high-tech new Dodge Grand Caravan, which the kids quickly christened The Green Hornet.

Because of stress brought on by a few incorrigible students, dysfunctional parents and picky, picky politically designed federal and state paper trails, I announced my retirement effective in June.

Shortly thereafter, they (a committee of my esteemed friends) couldn't have found worse pictures of me with which to roast me at my retirement party held at a nearby restaurant conference room and attended by 100 plus friends and relatives. They made slides and added comments providing us all, yes, even me, with considerable bouts of hilarity. Then it was announced that the Blues Brothers would be entertaining us with a song or two. Wow, those brothers certainly resembled a couple of my fellow teachers. Lastly, the floor was opened to ribald stories contributed by all whom I had encountered over the years. A few days later, I asked Kay, who had videotaped each person as they entered the room, asking each to give their name and how they knew me, for the tape so that I might not only know all who attended, but also so I could send thank you cards for their contribution to the money tree. Tape? The camera had been empty when she opened it. I was relegated to putting a letter in the local papers expressing my gratitude, not exactly an Emily Post bit of etiquette.

June also brought the announcement from the Goodalls that they were selling their lovely home and returning to Utah. I shall miss their ever-present help, but most of all their love and kindness.

Indecent exposure? Nudity? Applying for a job in a topless salon? Big, red, itchy bumps had appeared on my neck, shoulders and underarms. When they started being painful, I paid my doctor a visit. Diagnosis, shingles. All who have been blessed with this dreaded affliction know that anything touching the lesions only enhance the discomfort. Remedy, going without upper clothing. Also, the sun seemed to soothe. Relaxing on my patio in the country with no close neighbors, I felt I was safe from ogling eyes. Oh d..m, caught by the meter reader. I can just imagine I provided some laughs among his colleagues.

After a day of shopping in Longview, Lynda and I were a few miles from home when the van suddenly expired. Out of gas? No, the indicator showed the tank was over 1/2 full. What to do?? It was hot, and there was no room for me to exit van unless my desire was to end up in the ditch. I persuaded Lynda to hike to a business a short ways up the road, and call my mechanic, Marcello, to come rescue us. She had been gone a few minutes when a UPS driver stopped. I convinced him that help was on the way, but I did accept his offer of a cold can of Pepsi. Lynda returned with the proprietor of the business, who had a towrope, and he hauled us to his shop. Lynda positioned herself by the road to flag Marcello down. He didn't see her, observed that the van was no longer there, assumed she got it started, and returned to his garage. Another call and he was back, but he couldn't deduce the problem. A tow truck was engaged and the Hornet was hauled to the Dodge dealer who informed me that this high-tech van was truly out of gas; a faulty gas gauge was replaced.

My incredibly wild, mechanically, physically, mentally and socially challenged year is over. Therefore, I shall close by hoping that you have had a better year than me, your friend or relative.

Merry Christmas,

Shirley, retired

CHRISTMAS 1999

Hi from WWW (Wet Western Washington),

Close to spring break, and I was feeling hemmed in with too much rain, and decided if I didn't get away from it, I soon would be getting webbed feet, growing feathers and heading south. Aha! South??? Why not? After talking it over with Kay, it was decided south we would go. My friend, Pat, who had lost her husband and a son and was needing diversion, would go along even though she had two very sore legs. "She was leg wrestling?" you ask. No, she had taken a tumble at her attorney's office. Lawsuit? Do you think he'd take *that* case? She wasn't in the mood for lawyer-squabbling, so scratched that idea.

At six A.M. we were heading down I-5. Kay, bent on getting over the Siskiyou Mountains before dark, would not stop for lunch. As we picnicked in the van while moving, Kay made a quick turn and I did not. I was suddenly wearing my banana.

Radio on, we were warned that both passes we would cross required either snow tires or chains. We had neither. A stop at Les Schwab's in Medford, a purchase of chains, and we ventured on. What? No snow on the highway! Saved.

The night was spent in Redding, CA, where Pat was sure the sprinkler heads were little cameras spying on us. We attributed her apparitions to the meds she was taking for depression.

While zooming along, something got between my hard contact lens and my eye. Yow! It hurt. Pat was driving; Kay was in the back seat. I needed help as I had rubbed my eye resulting in the contact clinging to the upper part of my eye. Since we were nearing Sacramento, traffic was congested so pulling off the freeway was not an option. Can you imagine what went through the minds of fellow travelers when they saw this woman leaning over me poking at my eye as Kay tried to recenter the lens? Success! I could once again see with both eyes.

After a very long day, we arrived in Palm Springs, where we had reservations at a comfortable hotel.

With Jo as our tour guide, we saw but didn't swim in the Salton Sea, had lunch at a classy hotel which had a pool so large that it had gondoliers squiring fancy ladies around, visited a shop with only black dresses, then one with only white, where the prices would even shock Bill Gates, gambled $20 at a casino, had dinner at an authentic Mexican restaurant where even "mild" cuisine burned my gullet, and best of all, ate a campfire dinner with Matt and Jo at their vacation spot on the edge of PGA West's golf course.

Time for leave taking. We ate breakfast at IHOP. "Shirley, Shirley," I heard as we are leaving. Thinking it was some other Shirley, as who would know me there? I continued to head for the van. Some molester (wishful thinking) grabbed and smooched me before I could see who it was. Butch! A friend from home. Darn, foiled again. He was there visiting another transplant from our area.

We headed for home, with a stop in Medford to return chains. Not too useful in the rain. In Canyonville where we spent the night, I fed the slots at a casino another $20. WOW, I made $80, recovering my losses and sported us to a nice dinner. At breakfast at the motel, we found that the tables were full. A nice couple invited us to join them. We exchanged info. They were from Seattle. Kay told them we were from a small town few people are aware of. But they had. When the lady informed me she once had an aunt who lived there, and I heard the name, I gasped, "I knew her. She worked in our drug store." As they say, "small world."

Home. Always good to get away, but my bed sure felt good after lumpy mattresses and cramped quarters.

We had a lovely summer. Too hot for some, but not this sun worshipper. I'm now subbing at the high and middle schools, reading, pecking away on an outdated computer and getting ready for the holidays.

Hoping that Y2K doesn't mess up your life, I'm wishing you a very Merry Christmas,

Love to all, Shirley

CHRISTMAS 2000

Dear Family and Friends,

Upon retiring in 1998, I realized how dependent I had become on a computer as a dictionary, encyclopedia and for just about anything requiring writing. The school had some out-of-date computers sitting in a storeroom. Upon request, they donated one to me. However, this, too, was not sufficient for my needs. Therefore, I decided I must get out the credit card and go searching for a new, more reliable one. Since I was used to the Apple, it necessitated a trip to Portland to the Apple Store.

I arrived home with my new iMac and was excited to get it set up and going. I made a quick phone call to my computer expert, Chuck. In no time at all, he had it up and running, plus had transferred the old data to the new.

Three days later, my hard drive crashed from, of all things, a stuck-down key. Back to Portland where I was informed it couldn't be fixed. A new one in hand, back home we went where Chuck again got my address book, finances, and all other needed data transferred.

Two weeks later, I went to enter some info into my checking account to find there was no account there. Alyx and Amanda had been playing some games and had managed to DUMP everything from my account. Luckily I keep a paper trail, but it took a complete day to re-enter a year's worth of finances.

'Twas but a week later the disk drive crashed. A call to the Computer Store brought the UPS man to my door with a new drive that again was installed by Chuck.

About a month later a disk got caught in the drive. Neither Chuck nor the Apple men could get it out without damaging the computer. I went home with computer number three.

By this time, I was about ready to throw out the computer and go back to pen and paper. However the salesman, who by now was getting tired of me, agreed I deserved some type of gratuity for sticking with their product and sent me several new programs, my pick.

If this weren't bad enough, as I was getting flustered trying to figure out one of the new programs, my computer table did a nose dive and to the floor went computer, printer and external Zip drive. All I could think of was computer #4. But God must have been smiling that day. No damage but for big bruises on my legs from the table hitting them as it went down.

Through all of this, I lost my e-mail addresses, so if you haven't received any of my drivel, that is why. Please e-mail me so that I have them. For the last six months, no computer crashes. Hopefully, Mr. iMac and I will continue to coexist in harmony.

After all of the computer problems, I decided I needed to get away. However cash was short, my family reunion was coming up, and therefore, I needed to conserve. A few days later, my traveling friend, Bobbie, came to visit. "How would you like to go to Boston and NYC with me?" she inquired. "I'd love to. Never been to the east coast, but can't, no dollars." I replied. "You've got plastic. We'll share expenses, my Delta airline pilot brother can get us vouchers for $150, and we can hit your family reunion in Boise on the way home." I was easily convinced.

Plans were made. We would drive to Boise, leave the van with my brother, catch the plane and off we'd go on another Watson adventure. Delta didn't have a direct flight to Boston, which meant a change of planes in Salt Lake where I had some relatives that live nearby. Now planes are not my favorite mode of travel. Since I can't stand, to get through security, they have to have someone lift me up while they check under my cushion for the drugs, guns or explosives that I might be hiding. Then they bring the boarding chair. They no longer allow anyone but employees to transfer we w/c bound. I'm transferred into it (I'm wondering how they manage those much bigger than my 110 lb.), wheeled onto the plane first where I get dirty looks for cutting into the line and deposited into my seat. We arrived in SLC, I waited for all passengers to exit, two young men brought the boarding wheelchair which if I were an inch wider, I would not fit, tugged me into it (a feat at best for Superman) and out we went. They parked me in the waiting area while they went looking for my motorized w/c. Bobbie and I visited with the relatives. An hour later the guys appeared with chair intact (a miracle), and I was resettled again. Three hours later, the procedure was engaged again. We're off. We landed in Boston, same game only this time when my chair arrived, it had a broken leg/foot rest. What to do? Call w/c shops or cut off my leg? The latter seemed somewhat drastic, so Bobbie started checking out w/c sales. Not one of them had what I needed. A call to my guy in Portland assured me he'd overnight me one. We went to the airport claims department where they would only reimburse me for $100, the part is $250. Oh well, I have PLASTIC.

I then called Flying Wheels. The van that I had made arrangements to rent was not available. They sent a substitute. Not the best looking van, but it saved wheeling throughout New England in my chair. Bobbi's sister had graciously offered a bedroom for a home base while we did the tourist thing. However, at bedtime, we found she had had to rent cots for our sleeping. Not feasible for this quad. We found a 'not so great' motel with a vacancy. Upon arriving, we found it had two steps. We looked again. Finally at midnight, Bobbie spied a Day's Inn. Because they were so accommodating, we stayed at a Day's Inn whenever one was available.

Our week in New England was over too soon. Lobster was so cheap, compared to what we get on the West Coast, that we feasted on it. We had lobster dipped in butter, lobster sandwiches, lobster cakes, and any other way that it could be prepared. By the time we headed for NYC, we were surely growing claws.

We, along with Bobbie's sister Marybeth, entered NYC and sat for 45 minutes, while a van that was moving someone's belongings blocked the narrow street. We arrived at our hotel in the theater district. I had booked it on-line. It definitely did NOT live up to its ad. I had requested two "standard" beds. Apparently a "standard bed" to New Yorkers is a twin bed. There was no way three of us could accomplish the feat of two to one bed. Next room had the right beds, but it was so small I couldn't get my chair further than the open door. Room three was ok after they moved out all of the furniture but the beds. The chair had to be left in the hall, and my bathroom duties had to be performed in the small space left when the door was shut. In the a.m., Bobbie would get me taken care of, then shove me out the door so they could get in and out of said room.

Sightseeing in NYC was exceptional for this permanently seated woman. I got to go to the head of the lines; at the Empire State Building we got a special elevator, and theater tickets were not only $6 for me but my companion also. Instead of seeing the one play we had felt we could afford, we went to four. I wanted to eat at a typical Italian delicatessen. We found one not too far from our hotel. Upon ordering a bowl of split pea soup, it was served in what I would call a mixing bowl! Each of the gal's sandwiches would feed three. We passed on the plate-sized desserts. All too soon our three days were gone. I never got to see one museum, but maybe I can go another time for I have PLASTIC.

No mishaps on the return trip to the Boise family reunion and then home.

Merry Christmas and a happy and prosperous New Year.

Shirley

CHRISTMAS 2001

January brought some snow, which quickly disappeared, leaving only one day of school to make up. In February, as I was pecking out some e-mails at the computer, I suddenly realized that wheelchair and I were sliding across the room, braking to a stop as I hit my desk. No, the office floor does not tilt. Mother nature decided we had become too sedate in our existence and sent us an earthquake to shake us back into a more active life. No damage was done except to Lynda's nerves. She is not acquainted with our sporadic quakes.

I had been assigned to substitute for Chuck and decided my few gray hairs needed to be sent back to brown before I was once again among my teaching buddies. Lynda got out the dye and set to making all my locks brown. Yipes, when finished, I looked in the mirror. Not brown but blackish purple. Too late to do a makeover. All day long, my peers peeked into my classroom to see this usually modest woman in her Halloween make-up. I weathered their jokes with a regal pose.

In June my neice Darlene and I took a little trip to Arizona to see Dick and Delores. I made up a little poem to tell this tale. It goes:

> We entered Wickenburg
> Where we were told, Alas!
> You have a little problem,
> Your van is leaking gas.
>
> Old van problems clanged for me
> My spirits were not brightened.
> Until friend Dick laughed and said,
> No need to be frightened.

> Cars here in the desert don't like heat
> Their gas begins to expand
> Until they can no longer hold it in
> And they leak it onto the land.

Problem solved.

My niece, Susan, called to tell me they were going to be at Cannon Beach and would I come down to see them. After getting details of dates and place, Lynda and I headed out. What I had forgotten to do was get their room number at the motel. We were told they had checked in, but the desk clerk wouldn't give me the info I needed. She did call their room, no answer, but that was expected. Who would be sitting in their room on a sunny day at the beach? I was reduced to looking for a vehicle with Utah license plates. Yeah, what luck. It was in the first row of parked cars. We left a note on the windshield of the truck saying we were there and where we would be and headed for the restaurant next door. After waiting several hours, we decided to comb the crowded beach. It was getting late and we needed to leave and just then Susan appeared. What luck, but she informed me they had a van, not a truck. Therefore, we only had time for a short visit. One can only imagine what the owner of the truck thought when he read our note.

In September Fran, Jo and I decided it would be fun to take the train to Seattle to spend the day. I hadn't been on a train since the '50's when I would go to Denver each summer, and I was excited. But even a train ride didn't release me from my usual trip predicaments.

> Got my chair, got my reservation
> Spent each dime I could afford
> Got on board with anticipation
> When my battery power was lowered

Short time was all that I had left
Just a bit of power to go
Won't be able to leave the station
So I had to tell Fran and Jo.

Well before you could say 'All aboard'
The two of them started to plot
Lots of phone calls, lots of 'magination
Lots of laughs before they got

An expert wheelchair repairman
Who only took a little while
To tell me my chair was really ok
So we could finish our trip in style.

So we took our sentimental journey
Seems that everyone agrees
Didn't just renew old ones
But we made new memories.

When lying on my back in bed, I sometimes have my helper put my TV on a tray across my chest to pass away some boring hours. During one such occurrence, my leg did one of its acrobatic maneuvers causing the TV to flatten my face. No race to the doc was needed, but I did end up with a fat lip and a very sore nose.

The destruction of the twin towers and the pentagon make my trials diminish considerably. I never thought I'd see our beautiful, peaceful country attacked again by a foreign nation after Pearl Harbor. May I not live to see it again.

Out of tales, out of time and God bless the USA.

Happy New Year. Love, Shirley

CHRISTMAS 2002

In January, I was asked to move as the landlord's son wanted to move in. I searched for a place in which to park my belongings and me. My angel, Linda Breneman, bought a home down the road, with a huge, beautiful deck and large windows that overlook the high school with Mt. St. Helens in view. I rented it at a fee low enough to cover taxes and upkeep. Never again must I move, but it is a good way to get rid of rubbish. Teaching peers became my movers, ramp builders, cleaners and put awayers.

For the first time since post accident, I have a bathroom I can get into and even turn around. No more brushing teeth, donning makeup and styling my locks in the hallway.

The living room posed a problem; it was sunken. It was either entertain guests in the kitchen, and watch TV with a telescope or raise it up. Handy man, Barry, raised the floor, pulled up carpets from living, kitchen, bedroom, bath and halls and installed laminate wood floors. I'm also within wheeling range of schools and town. The only drawback, a huge landscaped yard to care for and five acres of hay but no animals to eat it.

My summer was spent supervising yard work, shepherding visitors on tours of St. Helens, taking a trip to Seattle to celebrate Dick and Delores Breneman's 50th anniversary, and then ditto for JoAnn and Wilmer Lyons in September.

Bang, bang on my door, then desperate yelling. There was a small fire on the edge of my hayfield. A neighbor had spotted it on her way to town. I called 911, she grabbed my hose, but it was not long enough and the fire was quickly spreading toward my neighbor's home. Someone spotted it from the school and several came with shovels and wet gunnysacks. By this time I was a blubbering mess. Finally the firemen came. Fire was contained, then out. Didn't I tell you fires were my nemesis? I just know the next one will consume me.

In November, Lynda got up, got kids off to school and then fell over. Dizzy to the point of being violently ill, she managed to crawl to the bathroom. I made another 911 call and one to our friend, Jo, who accompanied her to the hospital. Vertigo was the diagnosis. They kept her there for the night, and then home with pills, which put her back in A-1 shape.

Fall has been spent subbing, tutoring, and losing tan. But all are well and looking forward to the holidays.

Merry Christmas everyone.

Love from Meeee

CHRISTMAS 2003

Greetings,

A few excerpts from my joys of life in Toledo.

Eyes... Droopy eyelids lifted, doc claimed I had little lateral perception. I thought they made me look sexy. Cataract surgery on both eyes. Thirty-one visits to cataract clinic, hemorrhages, blood clots, lens leaks. I finally asked to have my name on the door as a major financial donor. Poor results. A seeing eye dog might be an option. I can't see leaves on the trees. Others tell me it is because it is winter. I question that theory. Left eye features curvy vision. If I were following the centerline while driving, I would get a DUI.

Further test at Oregon eye specialists... This one required me to have bright chartreuse dye injected into my veins. Testing chair was so slippery; I was beginning to think I was on a "slip and slide." Jo was enlisted to be my seat belt. I was warned that my urine would be a brilliant color, but I was not prepared for my blue eyes to turn green or my skin to turn chartreuse. Temporary alien? I caused a few stares in the waiting room.

Baby shower for Lynn... held in a room at the top of a long flight of stairs. I volunteered to sit in the van and read. Robin could give me details upon return. However, upon their insistence, I agreed to be carried. One grabbed under my arms, another one under my knees. By the time we got to the top, their hands had slipped to my wrists and ankles, my fanny was sweeping the floor clean and my bra was up around my neck. I accused them of trying to lynch me.

Podiatrist... I have a callus on my foot, which needs removing every two months. If he keeps doing that, I am going to become shorter than I already am.

Meds... Because of high prescription costs, I have been having a friend who winters in Southern California purchase them for me in Mexico at a much cheaper price. I'm in my second year of using them and close to speaking fluent Spanish.

Lynda... decided to practice her gymnastic skills on the stairway to the basement. She cried for help, but I could do nothing but call 911 AGAIN. If I keep this up, they are going to park an ambulance in my driveway. Diagnosis, sprained ankle. Since she is on crutches, she has to supervise 13-year-old Amanda in the fundamentals of quad care.

Sun bathing... On a day trip with friends, Fran and Jo, we visited an island in the Columbia River known for its organic produce. After filling the trunk with healthy vittles, we decided to further explore the island. About half way around the perimeter, we viewed a sign that read, "Bathing area, Clothing Optional." We decided organic veggies were enough; organic bodies would cause sunburned derrieres.

Another year has closed. Have a fabulous 2004, my family and friends...

Love, Shirley,

the almost nudist

CHRISTMAS 2004-2007

Because of some health problems for three years, I didn't get my usual Christmas letters sent. Plus, not much of interest has happened since, but I shall try including what laughable incidents have transpired during these years.

In 2006, I got new help. Not one but five. I had known Marcy from subbing at school and had asked her if she knew anyone who would work for me as my pal Sam had to quit because of a health problem. Marcy informed me that she would be my hands, but that she was responsible for her two younger brothers and a sister. After inquiring into the situation, I found out that their mother had deserted them three years earlier, their father lived in Mexico, and she and her boyfriend of three years had been caring for her siblings. Problem solved. They'd have a better home, and I'd not only have help, but also some mental stimulation. They are all great kids and get along amazingly well for their age differences, especially since they are living with 19-year-old sister/mother. I now have five slaves. Slave # 1 is Marcy, who cares for me and is in pre-nursing at a community college; Slave # 2 is Aaron, the boyfriend, 21, who works in landscaping and does some of my yard work; Slave # 3 is Alma, just turned 18, and who works in our hometown fast food joint and fills in for Marcy when necessary; Slave # 4, David, is 14, a freshman, quiet but a tease; and Slave #5, Danny, is 11, in the sixth grade and my go-for boy. They spoil me rotten. It is Marcy's fault that I have put ten pounds of butter on my tummy.

After three years of being in bed 90% of the time, with a small but deep dicubitus ulcer (bedsore), and 37 visits (chauffeured mainly by friend, JoAnn) to several specialists in Portland and Seattle who either tried to heal my wound from inside out, or stated I had to learn to live with it, I found a surgeon with great healing powers. He cut out scar tissue, sewed it up and, ole ! it was healed in TWO WEEKS. I owe that man my sanity.

I happened to see one of my former students this fall that made me think of a math placement test my aide, Sherri, was giving him. This is how it went:

Sherri... If I gave you a dime for every day of the week, how much would you have at the end of the week?

Student... That depends.

Sherri... Depends on what?

Student... If it was a five-day week or a ten-day week.

Sherri... Well, I can't tell you that.

Student... OK then. One dollar.

Needless to say, the student received a calendar lesson.

God bless and happy days ahead.

Love, Shirley, the bedbug

CHRISTMAS 2008

Greetings,

As usual, in the life of a quad, I can't be trusted to not have little mishaps invading my sanity every so often.

One day in early Jan., I was working on my computer when my whole %^&*$ table collapsed onto my lap; computer, telephone, cup of tea, printer, papers and other necessary paraphernalia landed on the floor. No sweating; therefore, no broken leg. I called my neighbor, Leslie. She remedied the situation with no damage done except for some lovely tea-stained papers. Needless to say, the table is now glued together rather than held with clips that connect one half into the other.

Another day, I leaned over (a little too far) to reach something and "whack" went my nose into the desk. Usually, I can get back up, but this time my headrest prohibited such a maneuver. The kids had just run to the store so the wait wasn't long. I wasn't so fortunate the second time... the kids were all at school! After trying to call all five of my neighbors without success, and contemplating on what I could fantasize on for the next three hours, I had to rely on calling Kay (my secretary friend at the middle school) to see if any teacher was on a break. She arrived herself. "Oh, I thought you had fallen out of your chair," she remarked. I asked her how she thought she'd get me back into it if I had.

The next calamity was not of my making. I had bought a new refrigerator. Sears had asked that the old one be removed from its niche before they brought the replacement. Because the old one had an icemaker, it was connected to a water pipe. Marcy thought she could just cut it off, not realizing water would still flow. OOPS. She couldn't find the shut-off valve. Thankfully, a neighbor was home to come to the rescue. Marcy now knows where the water shuts off.

Fire seems to be our nemesis, but water is our arch enemy. The water pump died recently. "The basement bath is flooded," Danny yelled. I called my friendly plumber (nice to know former students in the trades). The problem was behind the wall. Apparently, it had been leaking for some time. Marcy had been saying there was an odor downstairs, but she couldn't detect the source. She had been blaming her brothers for the stench.

In June, the kids and I pooled our resources and headed south. We stayed with relatives when possible and cheap motels otherwise. We visited the "Wild Life Safari" in Oregon, kid's grandparents in Redding, California, Reno where I gambled $20 and left with $27 (big spender), and had fun gabbing with brothers, nieces and nephews in Utah and Idaho. For the first time during my many auto excursions, we never left any money with a mechanic.

In August, we celebrated my first "Slave Day." "Slave Day" you ask? All my former helpers, both full-time and fill-ins, were invited for a BBQ. Twenty-two arrived, some with their families. Tears of laughter flowed from the "Shirley" stories.

Getting dressed one day, Marcy was pulling up my zipper, when her hand slipped and hit me in the eye. The next morning, I had a nice, big shiner. Elder abuse? You betcha. No one believed her story.

Other events: a surprise BD party given by my former high school friends, a trip to Seattle to shuttle relatives from their hotel to their cruise ship, isolation in Toledo for several days due to flooded highways north of us, and 29 here for Thanksgiving.

My little family is shrinking. Alma completed beauty school, turned 20 and decided it was time to be on her own. She is house-sitting, for now, for a former employer. She has a good job and loves her work. The others continue with their educations, and I am enjoying being back in circulation subbing at the High School and Middle School.

May this coming year, with a new government, bring all a renewed prosperity and relief from our down-sliding economy. Let's all pray for a brighter New Year. I am.

Love, Shirley

I was one of Toledo's "Big Cheeses" this year. That's code for "you're getting old and you've lived here a long time..."

The Family: David, Pickles the Cat, Aaron, Danny, Marcy, Me and Alma

CHRISTMAS 2009

Greetings from Plomondon Road,

My year did not start out well. In January, a precious niece died of a heart attack at age 45. In February, her mother, who was like a sister to me, was diagnosed with cancer and died a few days later. In between those two tragedies, I spent ten days in the hospital with pneumonia and kidney infection. All of these happened within 27 days. I'm canceling Jan. and Feb. in 2010. If you don't hear or see me during those months, it is because they don't exist.

The kids and I went on some short adventures in the spring and summer. We visited OMSI (Oregon Museum of Science and Industry) where we saw the replicas of da Vinci's inventions, amazing since he was way ahead of his time.

The Flight Museum in Seattle was another destination. The big attraction there, besides all of the airplanes, was the flight simulator. It takes two people to maneuver it---one to pilot it, the other to man the guns. After watching my kids twist, turn upside down and head for who knows where, I decided we would lose any war if they were at the controls of the fighter jets.

In August, we headed out to Spokane to visit niece Tanya, with a stop in Yakima to have lunch with Roxann, and also took a side trip to Silverwood, the largest amusement park in the NW, 30 miles outside of Spokane in northern Idaho. I people-watched and talked to other people-watchers while the kids waited in lines for 20-30 minutes to have their heads plummet into their stomachs for a 'two minute' ride which they exited with purple faces and collapsed lungs. Then we traveled SW to the Tri-Cities where we had BBQ with my niece, Darlene, and family, spent the night and returned home.

Twice this year, I've exited my van and was not able to re-enter. My ramp refused to deploy. Somewhere in the mechanism it seems to get a short, and it refuses to listen no matter the amount of kicking and cursing we do. The emergency release is something that only Rube Goldberg would design. Not too difficult to release, but restoring it to its place of origin takes five arms and a litany of unmentionable words.

It apparently is time for a hearing aid. This morning some friends were visiting. Susie said something, and I replied with, "My ass burns most of the time." After they quit laughing Susie commented, "I said, take aspirin at bedtime." Oh, well, I'm always good to amuse others so why ruin it by purchasing the device?

Which reminds me... Danny and David love to try and shock me with naughty words and stories...their favorite, leaving pictures of the male genitalia around the house. One day while shopping, people kept giving me strange looks. I checked my face, no unusual problem there, clothes were clean and intact and my chair seemed to be working properly. It wasn't until I returned home that I found one of those male gender pictures taped on the back of my w/c. The brats! I got them back though. We were celebrating Danny's birthday with dessert at a nearby restaurant. The boys had ordered something that came with a cherry on top which neither wanted. ""Shirley, do you want this cherry?" David asked. "No, I lost mine a long time ago and don't plan on replacing it." I replied. Their faces turned a brighter red than the cherry. Enough said.

We have a new baby in the house via Alma, 28 bodies to feed and entertain for Thanksgiving and shopping left to do then; alas, in a few days the year will have come to its final resting place.

God bless and MERRY CHRISTMAS

Shirley

CHRISTMAS 2010

For my birthday, the kids took me to Fugiyama's, a Japanese restaurant in Olympia where a chef who thinks he is a standup comic cooks your choice of Surf or Turf on a grill in front of you and is constantly shoving it onto your plate. While the kids sat on stools, my chair refused to fit under the 5' counter. It was either sit sideways and scoop the food from plate to mouth where more than likely I'd miss my choppers and subsequently have to eat it off my lap OR put the plate on my lap and hope that I could leave the place without wearing my food as a coat. During the meal, Danny, age 14, kept leaving for the potty room. I assumed it was because he had downed several large glasses of cola, but he informed me that it wasn't that organ he was evacuating but one further back on his derriere. He swore the drink lady was putting Ex-Lax in his drink. That statement brought forth more laughter than what the "comic" provided.

For a doctor's appointment, Marcy pulled into the nearest space in the parking garage and we departed. I was there to have some tests to find the source of my continuous daytime pain that is indicated by sweats. These ceased to exist at night leaving me to surmise that after 55 years of sitting, my fanny was yelling "help me." A couple of hours later, I was free of pokes, punches and x-rays, and we wormed our way through the torture chamber and out to the garage. Going at my usual racing speed, I reached the van before Marcy emerged through the door. I patiently waited for her arrival, which was slow in coming. Finally, I heard her little voice saying, "Shirley, what are you doing?" as she poked her head around the back of the van. "Just waiting for you," I impatiently replied. "I'm not sure you can get into THAT van," she laughed. Oh well, it was the same make, model and color, but minus the gold wheels and ramp door. I could have claimed the tests had affected my eyesight, but doubt she would have believed that since the tests were on the other end.

One of those days of misery, the only thing that sounded good to eat was soup. I asked Marcy to heat some good ole Campbell's tomato, but to make it a little more interesting, I asked her to add a few small chunks of cheese. Apparently she didn't hear the 'small' part of the request as she had enough cheese in it to plug up the hole in Hans Christian Anderson's dike. I won't mention what it did to mine.

The tests had failed to reveal any oddities other than the ones I was born with. We were perplexed and after many months of reclining in my office cell watching non-entertaining TV, Marcy stated she was going to put a couple pumps of air into my w/c cushion. Several times earlier, I had asked her to sit in my chair to test the air flow which she assured me was fine. She went about the procedure, plunked me in the chair and I prepared for another day of boredom. After performing my morning ablutions, I set about checking my e-mail that usually ended up with rivulets of perspiration running into my wrinkles and dripping off the end of my snout. One hour later, no sweats, two hours passed, still no moisture, three, four, five etc. Either my body had said "no more reclining" or the puffs of air had performed miracles that the x-ray, CT scan and prodding could not. It was apparent that Marcy testing the cushion for two minutes was different than my fanny sitting on it for hours. At last I was pardoned and released from prison. I could now go about living in the outside world.

The Green Hornet has been a super reliable piece of machinery. It has taken me south to Mexico, north to Canada and a zillion other sites far and near, but after 12 years of service, it decided this summer that enough was enough. After all, in human years, it is 100. Over the ages, the poor thing has had the undercarriage run over speed bumps (remember it sits much lower to the ground than its normal counterparts), and caught on curbs etc. On one blissful morning this summer, I asked David to go start the Hornet as we were heading off on a shopping spree.

"What the heck is that?" I screamed. "We're being invaded by a battalion of Taliban tanks?" I rushed to the garage to see a stream of blue testosterone shooting out of the Hornet's tail and his belching roar making the walls quiver. A new muffler and tail pipe alleviated his complaints.

It was just a few weeks later as a friend and I were returning from town; I deduced that the Hornet had caught a cold as he was shivering uncontrollably. I called on my friend, Kim, who knows machines, to investigate the problem. In my mental file, I have all of my emergency friends' phone numbers. Kim is one of those. He is like a s'more; rough and tough on the outside, sweet and gooey on the inside. But always there for me in divining contraption problems. "No cold," he pointed out. The Hornet had just lost one of his wheel marbles. Right back to Campbell's Dodge menders he was taken to get his marble back in place along with a new heart.

In the fall, Marcy informed me she and the rest of her little family were moving. It was going to be too hard for her to care for the house, while having to be at the hospital at 5:30 AM to continue with her RN training and me. She had already found me a replacement, a high school girl, Samantha, who prefers to be called Sam. David is here during the day helping me with those little piddling things that drive me bonkers; ie, dropped pencils, feet getting out of control, food receptacle complaining it needs filling and being yanked back up when I try to be Plastic Man reaching beyond my range. The kids just moved about two blocks away as the crow flies so we either see each other, or at least talk each day. However, the house is too, too quiet.

In my worst nightmares I never dreamed I'd be awakened by a cat chewing on my toes. But there was Sam's cat, Pickles, gnawing away at what I assumed he thought was a mouse under those covers. My autonomic dysreflexia had kicked in causing my legs to act like a kangaroo hopping on a prickly pear, jarring me from dreamland. A stream of yelling did not dissuade Pickles, and by this time I was hoping this pickle would drown in his brine. More screeching brought Sam to the rescue, but leaving a pool of blood behind on the sheets.

And that, my dears, is the end of my year's tale.
Happy Days Ahead,

Shirley

Some of Toledo's most influential people...

Acknowledgements

I wish to thank Linda Breneman for her encouragement and financial support; my niece, Tanya, for designing my web page, book cover and interior and help with publishing; Susan Greenwood for editing; my niece, Darlene, for gathering photos and proofreading; my good friends the Brenemans and Bonds, who have given me respite periods; my traveling companions, Bobbie Rieder and Jo Gefre; my pals and problem solvers, Chuck Caley, Fran Grove, Dorothy Nootenboom, Kay Lyon and Jack Rasmussen; my handymen, Mel Roeder, Guy Buswell, John Ball and Barry Taylor; my chauffeur, JoAnn Lyon; my "girls" who took such good care of me and who also became "my" kids along with Teddy, Erik, David, Danny, Alma and Aaron; and especially my family who refused to treat me as a handicapped woman. Without these and my many devoted friends, this book would not have been possible.

www.ingramcontent.com/pod-product-compliance
Lightning Source LLC
Chambersburg PA
CBHW060517100426
42743CB00009B/1358